SLAM DUNK!

The Top 10 Lists of *Everything* in
BASKETBALL

Sports Illustrated Kids

Managing Editor Mark Bechtel
Creative Director Beth Power Bugler
Director of Photography Marguerite Schropp Lucarelli

Created by 10Ten Media

Managing Directors Bob Der, Scott Gramling, Ian Knowles
Creative Director Anthony Scerri
Writer Zachary Cohen
Associate Editor Nina Pantic
Reporter Corinne Cummings

Time Home Entertainment
Publisher Jim Childs
Vice President, Finance Vandana Patel
Executive Director, Marketing Services Carol Pittard
Executive Director, Retail & Special Sales Tom Mifsud
Executive Director, Marketing Susan Hettleman
Executive Publishing Director Joy Bomba
Director, Bookazine Development & Marketing Laura Adam
Publishing Director Megan Pearlman
Assistant General Counsel Simone Procas
Assistant Director, Special Sales Ilene Schreider
Senior Book Production Manager Susan Chodakiewicz
Brand Manager Jonathan White
Associate Prepress Manager Alex Voznesenskiy
Associate Project Manager Stephanie Braga

Editorial Director Stephen Koepp
Senior Editor Roe D'Angelo
Copy Chief Rina Bander
Design Manager Anne-Michelle Gallero
Editorial Operations Gina Scauzillo

Special thanks: Katherine Barnet, Brad Beatson, Jeremy Biloon, Rose Cirrincione, Assu Etsubneh, Mariana Evans, Christine Font, Hillary Hirsch, David Kahn, Jean Kennedy, Amy Mangus, Kimberly Marshall, Nina Mistry, Dave Rozzelle, Ricardo Santiago, Holly Smith, Adriana Tierno

ISBN 10: 1-61893-129-6
ISBN 13: 978-1-61893-129-0
Library of Congress Control Number: 2014939722

Sports Illustrated Kids is a trademark of Time Inc.

We welcome your comments and suggestions about Sports Illustrated Kids Books. Please write to us at:
   Sports Illustrated Kids Books
   Attention: Book Editors
   P.O. Box 11016
   Des Moines, IA 50336-1016

If you would like to order any of our hardcover Collector's Edition books, please call us at 1-800-327-6388 (Monday through Friday, 7 a.m.–8 p.m., or Saturday, 7 a.m.–6 p.m., Central Time).

1 TLF 14

The San Antonio Spurs' David Robinson, shown here winning the opening tip-off against the New York Knicks in Game 5 of the 1999 NBA Finals, is one of the 10 greatest big guys of all time.

Before he joined the Brooklyn Nets prior to the 2013–14 season, Paul Pierce had enough clutch moments as a Boston Celtic to land him on the Top 10 list that begins on page 50.

THE TOP 10 LISTS

★★★ TOP 10 ★★★
GREATEST PLAYERS

1 LeBron James

The NBA has never had a player like LeBron James. Coming out of St. Vincent-St. Mary High School in Akron, Ohio, the hometown Cleveland Cavaliers made James the first pick of the 2003 draft. He delivered immediately, winning Rookie of the Year honors. He soon made the Cavs into a contender despite a weak supporting cast. The franchise made its first Finals appearance in 2007. LeBron won his first MVP award in 2008–09.

At 6'8" and 260 pounds, James is built like a power forward, but he has the explosiveness and quickness normally found in a point guard. James says he's capable of winning the scoring title every season, and he's probably right. But his tremendous court vision, combined with his physical skills (he throws off-balance cross-court passes that no one else can) make him as great a playmaker as the NBA has ever seen. Defensively, he's capable of guarding all five positions. It was James who shut down San Antonio Spurs star point guard Tony Parker in the 2013 Finals.

James jumped ship to join Dwyane Wade, Chris Bosh, and the Miami Heat in 2010, and with two stars supporting him he became unstoppable. He won two titles in his first three seasons with Miami. And he's shown no signs of slowing down.

Michael Jordan

There's a reason today's great players are now measured against Jordan. He was unstoppable during the 1990s due to a combination of athleticism and skill, but also because of his incredible competitive drive. He was relentless attacking once he found an opponent's weakness. And no one was better in the biggest games. He led the Chicago Bulls to six titles, taking home Finals MVP honors each time. The five-time MVP is the NBA's all-time leader in career scoring average (30.1).

3 Bill Russell

The one stat that defines Russell's greatness: 10 fingers, 11 rings. The 6' 10" center changed the way the NBA valued defense. In the 1950s, big men were expected to dominate games on the offensive end. A five-time MVP, Russell did it primarily through defense and rebounding. He was as smart as he was strong down low. He not only blocked shots, but he consistently kept the ball inbounds, deflecting them to himself or to a teammate so the Celtics gained possession. He understood angles and anticipated where rebounds would come off. He turned a Boston Celtics franchise that had never won a title into what many believe to be the greatest dynasty in any sport.

4 Magic Johnson

Magic was exactly that with the ball in his hands. The 6' 9" point guard was the engine that made the "Showtime" Lakers of the 1980s go. He was the rare player who combined both style and substance, his fast-breaking, no-look passes baffling defenders while dazzling fans. His greatness was apparent right from the start. As a rookie, he helped the Lakers reach the 1980 Finals. L.A. had a chance to clinch the title in Game 6, but would have to do it with star center Kareem Abdul-Jabbar out with an ankle injury. Johnson moved to center to start the game, and played forward and guard throughout the course of the night. He finished with 42 points, 15 rebounds, and seven assists in the win, and was named Finals MVP. He'd eventually lead the Lakers to five titles, winning three regular-season MVPs and three Finals MVPs along the way.

5 Wilt Chamberlain

Wilt the Stilt's single-game scoring record, 100 points against the New York Knicks on March 2, 1962, is a feat that may never be matched. Playing for the Philadelphia Warriors, he set single-season records for scoring average (50.4 in 1961–62) and rebounding (27.2 in '60–61). While he didn't have the same team success that Bill Russell did while winning 11 NBA titles for the Boston Celtics, Chamberlain did win championships with both the Philadelphia 76ers (1966–67) and Los Angeles Lakers (1971–72). He remains the most dominant offensive big man in the history of the game.

6 Larry Bird

Bird was a remarkable shooter. He was the best ever at making contested jumpers, not to mention a three-time NBA Three-Point Shootout champion. But the reason Larry Legend is on this list is because he did *everything* well. His basketball savvy was unmatched, whether it was setting up a teammate with a pass no one else saw coming or anticipating an opponent's next move on the defensive end of the court. A three-time MVP, he was the only player in league history to average more than 20 points, 10 rebounds, and five assists for his career. But most of all, he was the heart of a Boston Celtics team that won three titles.

7 Oscar Robertson

Robertson was a bit like the LeBron James of the 1960s, a do-it-all floor general who, at 6'5" and 220 pounds, posed a big matchup problem for opponents. His statistics during his time with the Cincinnati Royals were remarkable. He *averaged* a triple-double in 1961–62 (30.5 points, 12.5 rebounds, 11.4 assists), just his second season in the league, and nearly repeated the feat when he won league MVP in '63–64. Injuries were slowing Robertson by the time he was traded to the Milwaukee Bucks before the '70–71 season. Teaming up with Lew Alcindor (later known as Kareem Abdul-Jabbar), the Bucks won their only title in franchise history that season.

8 Kareem Abdul-Jabbar

Abdul-Jabbar's career resumé is as impressive as anyone's: He scored more points (38,387), won more NBA MVP awards (six), and played in more All-Star games (19) than any player in league history. A great athlete standing 7' 2", he came into the NBA as Lew Alcindor — he changed his name to Kareem Abdul-Jabbar after leading the Milwaukee Bucks to their only NBA title, in 1970–71. He later teamed up with Magic Johnson on the "Showtime" Los Angeles Lakers and won five more titles. Abdul-Jabbar ended his career with the most points in NBA playoff history (5,762), a mark that has since been topped only by Michael Jordan.

9 Tim Duncan

Since entering the NBA in 1997–98, Duncan has been the model of consistency for the NBA's most consistent franchise. He's labeled the greatest power forward in NBA history, winning four NBA titles and leading his Spurs past star-studded teams like Shaquille O'Neal and Kobe Bryant's L.A. Lakers, and LeBron James's Cleveland Cavaliers. He averaged at least 20 points and 10 rebounds in each of his first eight seasons. Through 2013–14, the Spurs had won 50 games every year of Duncan's career, with the exception of the lockout-shortened '98–99 season (in which they went 37–13, a pace for 61 wins if it was a full season).

10 Kobe Bryant

Ever since Michael Jordan hung up his sneakers for good, fans and the media have been looking for the "next Jordan." No one since His Airness has been more unstoppable inside the three-point arc, or more relentlessly competitive, than Bryant. Like the Chicago Bulls legend, Bryant mastered a Jordan-esque fadeaway and has been cold-blooded in late-game situations. Early in his career, he won three NBA titles as Shaquille O'Neal's sidekick on the Los Angeles Lakers. When Shaq left, the Lakers became Bryant's team, and he went on to lead them to two more championships.

Top 10 Teams

1. 1995–96 Chicago Bulls

The rest of the NBA was enjoying life without Michael Jordan. After leading the Bulls to three straight titles, Jordan retired before the '93–94 season to pursue a baseball career. The Bulls were still good, winning 55 games and a playoff series that season. Jordan returned midway through the '94–95 season, looking rusty as the Bulls fell to Orlando in the second round of the playoffs. The next season, His Airness was his old self. Scottie Pippen, now a superstar in his own right, was in his prime. Do-it-all sixth man Toni Kukoc was a perfect fit, as was newly acquired rebounding machine Dennis Rodman. Hall of Fame coach Phil Jackson melded them perfectly, and the result was a record 72 regular-season wins. The Bulls rolled to an NBA title and earned the right to call themselves the greatest team of all time.

2. 1971–72
Los Angeles Lakers

It had been 12 years since the Lakers moved from Minneapolis to Los Angeles, and they had yet to bring a title to L.A. They had acquired dominant big man Wilt Chamberlain on the cheap after the superstar demanded a trade from Philadelphia. But when knee problems forced star forward Elgin Baylor to retire nine games into the season, it looked like more disappointment was on the way. The Lakers won their first game after Baylor's retirement. They won their next 32, too, a record win streak that still stands today. Behind Chamberlain, "Mr. Clutch" Jerry West, and Gail Goodrich, the Lakers rolled to a 69-win regular season. After dropping Game 1 of the NBA Finals, they beat the New York Knicks four straight times for L.A.'s first NBA title in dominant fashion.

3. 1966–67
Philadelphia 76ers

Even with superstar Wilt Chamberlain, the Sixers had yet to win a title. Boston had beaten them in the playoffs each of the last two seasons, as Celtics big man Bill Russell held Chamberlain in check. New head coach Alex Hannum had a plan. Instead of relying only on Chamberlain, he emphasized passing. Chamberlain averaged 24.1 points that season, the first time he had ever averaged fewer than 33.5 in a season. But he also averaged a career-high 7.8 assists. Six different Sixers averaged double-digit points. They were 46–4 at one point, and finished with a then-record 68 wins. In the playoffs, Philly cruised past Boston in five games behind the balanced scoring of Chamberlain, Hal Greer, and Chet Walker. They beat the San Francisco Warriors in the Finals, finishing a total team effort with a title.

4. 1985–86
Boston Celtics

The Boston Celtics are basketball's greatest franchise, and this was the best team they ever had. Boston won the 1983–84 title behind four future Hall of Famers: forwards Larry Bird and Kevin McHale, center Robert Parish, and guard Dennis Johnson. But after losing to the Los Angeles Lakers in the 1985 Finals, it seemed something was missing. They found it in Bill Walton, a former league MVP who many thought was washed up. The Celtics offered the perfect role for Walton, coming off the bench as a versatile big man. While Bird won MVP honors for the third straight season, Walton was the NBA's Sixth Man of the Year. Boston went 67–15 during the regular season. Amazingly, including the playoffs, they went 50–1 in home games. The C's lost only three playoff games while outscoring opponents by more than 10 points per game.

5.1999–2000
Los Angeles Lakers

Despite having the NBA's best big man in Shaquille O'Neal and All-Star Glen Rice, one of the NBA's premier shooters, the Lakers were swept out of the playoffs for a second straight year in 1999. The jump from good team to great team was because of Kobe Bryant. Bryant often played out of control at times during his first three seasons, especially in the playoffs. He matured into a star in his fourth season. Kobe and Shaq formed an unstoppable 1–2 punch under the guidance of coaching legend Phil Jackson. L.A. won 67 games during the regular season, and O'Neal took home MVP honors for both the regular season and the NBA Finals. L.A. clinched the title with a comeback win over the Indiana Pacers in Game 6 of the Finals, with O'Neal scoring 41 points and Bryant adding 26. It was the first of three consecutive NBA Championships.

7.1982–83
Philadelphia 76ers

NBA MVP Moses Malone was asked how his team, which had won 65 games in the regular season, would do in the playoffs. His response: "fo', fo', fo'." He meant Philly would win the three playoff series needed to win a title, each in a four-game sweep. He was off, but not by much. Behind All-Stars Malone, Julius Erving, Maurice Cheeks, and Andrew Toney, plus Sixth Man of the Year Bobby Jones, the Sixers swept the New York Knicks, then jumped out to a 3–0 series lead over the Milwaukee Bucks. They slipped up in Game 4 before finishing off the Bucks in five. It set up a Finals matchup with the Los Angeles Lakers, who had beaten them in the 1980 and '82 Finals. The Sixers trailed at halftime in Games 1 through 4, and came back to win comfortably each time. It wasn't quite "fo', fo', fo'," but it was one of the NBA's greatest playoff runs of all time.

9.2012–13
Miami Heat

The Heat won their first title with the "Big Three" of LeBron James, Dwyane Wade, and Chris Bosh in 2011–12. But that season was cut short because of a labor dispute. Many thought the Heat would have to prove themselves over an 82-game season to be considered great. They did. In '12–13, Miami won 66 games during the regular season, which included a 27-game winning streak, the second-longest in NBA history. Their 12 double-digit wins in the postseason were the most ever, but the playoffs were still a grind. In Game 6 of the Finals, they were down five in the final minute against the San Antonio Spurs. But key threes by James and Ray Allen forced overtime, and the Heat eventually prevailed. They won a tightly contested Game 7 to clinch a second straight title. Miami proved that, like any great team, they could grind out the tough wins.

6.2007–08
Boston Celtics

Great teams need more than just talent. They need chemistry. When a team acquires a new star or two during the offseason, they can often start the season playing poorly. That was not the case with the 2007–08 Celtics. After winning just 24 games the previous season, Boston traded several young players and draft picks to acquire superstar Kevin Garnett and All-Star Ray Allen in separate deals. Garnett's defense and Allen's smooth shooting stroke meshed perfectly with crafty scorer Paul Pierce. Along with rising young point guard Rajon Rondo, the pieces fit perfectly. Boston won 66 games in the regular season and battled through a long postseason; each series went at least six games. The Celtics' most impressive victory was the one that clinched the title: they beat the Los Angeles Lakers, 131–92, in Game 6 of the NBA Finals.

8.1970–71
Milwaukee Bucks

The Bucks were instant contenders. In 1969–70, the franchise's second season in existence, they won 56 games. That's because they had drafted Lew Alcindor (who later changed his name to Kareem Abdul-Jabbar), a big man so dominant he is still the NBA's all time leading scorer. To get over the top the following season, they traded for another all-time great: Oscar Robertson. "The Big O" was aging but still a star, and the Bucks had one of the greatest combos ever. Alcindor won his first scoring title and first MVP award, while Robertson was an All-Star again. The Bucks won 66 games, which included a then-record 20-game winning streak. They lost only two games in the playoffs, outscoring opponents by more than 14 points per game. They swept the Baltimore Bullets in the NBA Finals, clinching a title in just the franchise's third season.

10.1986–87
Los Angeles Lakers

The Lakers won five world titles during the "Showtime" era, and this was their best team. Magic Johnson was in his prime, and an aging Kareem Abdul-Jabbar still had some gas left in the tank. More importantly, they had one of the best supporting casts in league history. James Worthy was a fellow future Hall of Famer who thrived running the floor. Lockdown defender Michael Cooper was the NBA's Defensive Player of the Year, Byron Scott was a top long-range specialist, and they had blue-collar bangers in A.C. Green and Kurt Rambis — there were no weaknesses on this team. For the second time in three years, the Lakers beat the rival Boston Celtics in a six-game NBA Finals. Johnson took a page out of Abdul-Jabbar's book in a Game 4 thriller, making a hook shot to win it. Magic was named Finals MVP after averaging 26.2 points and 13.0 assists.

HAIRSTYLES

★ TOP 10 ★

1 Ben Wallace

Wallace's relentless defense, combined with his unique afro hairstyle, inspired the phrase "Fear the Fro." Opponents had reason to be afraid: Wallace's domination in the paint helped the Detroit Pistons win the 2003–04 title.

2 Chris Andersen

Known as Birdman, Andersen has always been easy to spot on the basketball court. His huge mohawk goes along perfectly with the elaborate tattoos that cover nearly his entire body.

3 Kenny Walker
No player in NBA history rocked the flattop as well as Kenny "Sky" Walker. These days, players like Iman Shumpert are trying to revive the style.

4 Allen Iverson
Iverson's signature haircut — cornrows — inspired a league-wide trend in the 2000s. When he got rid of them 13 years later, it was major news.

5 Dwayne Schintzius
You might not think that a journeyman who played for six different teams over eight seasons could make much of an impact. But Schintzius's mullet, which he called "The Lobster," was one of the league's most famous haircuts.

6 Dennis Rodman
Known for his wild style on and off the court, "The Worm" often had multi-colored hair. The cheetah style might have been his most original look.

7 Andrew Bynum
In his lone season with the Philadelphia 76ers, Bynum didn't play a single minute because of injury. He did, however, spark conversation off the court when he decided to sport the perm/bowl combination on the bench.

8 Joakim Noah
Noah embodies the hard-nosed style of the Chicago Bulls. He also pulls off one of the league's most unique hairstyles: a long, flowing mane held together in a ponytail that he wraps up in a bun that sits atop his head.

9 Ron Artest
Artest legally changed his name to Metta World Peace, and nobody thought much of it. Maybe that's because he had hair like this, seemingly inspired by R&B artist Sisqo.

10 Drew Gooden
Gooden had a surprise for anyone thinking he was bald. It turns out he was hiding a little patch of hair on the back of his head all along!

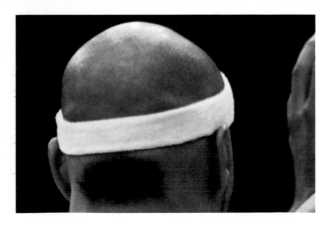

INTERNATIO STARS

1 Dirk Nowitzki
Germany

Nowitzki averaged only 8.2 points per game as a 20-year-old rookie in 1998–99. But Hall of Fame coach Don Nelson knew he had something special in the Dallas Mavericks' 7-footer with the kind of shooting touch and smarts that can't be taught. Nowitzki became a superstar, making the All-Star Game 11 straight times. He also brought the Mavericks their only title in franchise history, leading Dallas past the Miami Heat in the 2011 Finals.

2 Tony Parker
France

Parker's father, Tony Parker Sr., grew up in Chicago but played professionally in France, where Parker Jr. was raised. Selected by the San Antonio Spurs with the 28th and final pick of the first round in the 2001 NBA draft, he has helped the Spurs to 50-plus wins every season since he entered the league. He's also a three-time NBA champion, and in 2007 took home Finals MVP honors when the Spurs swept the Cleveland Cavaliers to win the title.

3 Yao Ming
China

At 7' 6", Yao was a huge presence in the NBA, but it went beyond what he did on the court. The big man was basketball's first Asian superstar, and his success had a huge impact for a sport that has grown worldwide. The top overall pick of the 2002 draft, Yao developed into a franchise player for the Houston Rockets, averaging 19.0 points and 9.2 rebounds and making the All-Star team in each of his eight seasons.

4 Pau Gasol
Spain

The Memphis Grizzlies saw Gasol as a franchise player in the 2001 draft, trading rising star Shareef Abdur-Rahim to Atlanta for the rights to him. He rewarded Memphis with three straight playoff berths, the first in franchise history. But Gasol's biggest impact came after he was traded to the Los Angeles Lakers during the 2007–08 season. He and Kobe Bryant led the Lakers to back-to-back titles in 2009 and '10.

5 Manu Ginobili
Argentina

The Argentine guard was playing in Italy when the San Antonio Spurs decided to spend the second-to-last pick of the 1999 draft on him. Since joining the Spurs three seasons later, the lefty has established himself as one of the craftiest players in the NBA. His Euro step — driving, picking up the ball, then changing direction with each of his two steps — is an offensive move that's now imitated throughout the league.

6 Drazen Petrovic
Croatia

The Portland Trail Blazers drafted Petrovic in 1986, and three years later he decided it was time to test himself against the world's best. After a season and a half as a reserve in Portland, he was traded to the New Jersey Nets, where Petrovic averaged 20 points per game during the '91–92 and '92–93 seasons. Traveling during a tour with the Croatian national team in 1993, Petrovic died in a car accident. He was only 28 years old.

7 Vlade Divac
Serbia

A 7-footer, Divac was light on his feet, an adept passer, and had a great midrange jumpshot. Replacing the legendary Kareem Abdul-Jabbar as the Los Angeles Lakers' center, he anchored the L.A. frontcourt during the early '90s before doing the same for the Charlotte Hornets and the Sacramento Kings. He finished his 16-year career as one of only six players to collect 13,000 points, 9,000 rebounds, 3,000 assists, and 1,500 blocked shots.

8 Peja Stojakovic
Serbia

The Sacramento Kings held a party for their fans during the 1996 draft. When the team drafted Stojakovic, the crowd was silent. "If you had to sum up the reaction in one word, it'd be: Who?" said one team official. After Stojakovic joined the team for the '98–99 season, fans learned who he was. Over 13 seasons, Stojakovic was a three-time All-Star who averaged 17.0 points per game and won the Three-Point Shootout in both 2002 and '03.

9 Toni Kukoc
Croatia

When Kukoc joined the Bulls in '93–94, his versatile skill set was a rarity in the NBA. He was 6' 11", but could shoot, handle, and pass like a guard. He averaged double-digit points in each of his six full seasons with Chicago, and won Sixth Man of the Year honors in '95–96. The Bulls won three consecutive NBA titles in the only three full seasons that Michael Jordan, Scottie Pippen and Kukoc played together.

10  Arvydas Sabonis
Lithuania

Sabonis is one of only 12 players born outside the U.S. to be inducted in the Basketball Hall of Fame. The Lithuanian big man earned the honor mostly due to his play in Europe during the 1980s and '90s, when he led the Soviet Union to a gold medal at the 1988 Olympics. The Portland Trail Blazers drafted the 7' 3" Sabonis in 1986, but he didn't make his NBA debut until '95–96, as a 30-year-old rookie.

NAL

TOP 10 COOLEST

1 Denver Nuggets (1982–83 to '92–93)
During the 1980s and early '90s, the Nuggets had one of the NBA's most colorful looks. Their uniforms featured the Denver skyline laid on top of a rainbow of stripes, honoring their home city in a funky way. The team's alternate gold jerseys, introduced before the 2012–13 season, pay homage to this classic look.

2 Toronto Raptors (1995–96 to '98–99)
The expansion Toronto Raptors brought a unique look to the NBA in the mid-'90s. The team debuted with white "Dino" jerseys at home and purple ones on the road. The look became a fan favorite, and the Raptors decided that they would wear them as throwbacks during the 2014–15 season.

3 Atlanta Hawks (1970–71 to '71–72)
Those who are used to seeing red in the Hawks' jerseys might be surprised to see what they looked like in the early '70s. Atlanta wore a lime green alternate uniform that featured a blue stripe going from the left shoulder to the bottom right of the matching shorts. The back of the jerseys had the player name *under* the number.

4 Milwaukee Bucks (1995–96 to '98–99)
The Bucks got back to nature with the alternate jerseys they introduced in the mid-'90s. The forest green jerseys featured a large graphic in the middle: a realistic buck with a menacing look. The team scrapped the look after four seasons, but re-introduced them as throwbacks prior to the start of the 2013–14 season.

5 Portland Trail Blazers (2009–10 to present)
Despite some nice looking regular uniforms, the Trail Blazers decided to experiment for the '09–10 season. They debuted a special alternate uniform featuring "Rip City," Portland's nickname, on the front. They were so popular with fans that the Blazers decided to keep them around.

JERSEYS

6 **Philadelphia 76ers (1991–92 to '93–94)**

The 76ers decided to do something unique in the early '90s, creating one of the busiest looking uniforms the league has ever seen. The "Sixers" nickname was made to look like it was flying out of the players' shorts, leaving a trail of multi-colored stars behind it.

7 **Houston Rockets (1995–96 to 2002–03)**

After winning back-to-back NBA Championships in 1994 and '95 in their traditional red-and-gold jerseys, the Rockets switched to navy blue road uniforms with vertical white pinstripes. The logo featured an angry-faced rocket circling a basketball; the logo and uniforms were scrapped after eight seasons.

8 **Utah Jazz (1996–97 to 2003–04)**

After featuring purple and gold uniforms for a decade, the Jazz switched to unique jerseys featuring an icy blue mountain logo. These jerseys were worn during the team's back-to-back trips to the NBA Finals in 1996 and '97, behind the Hall of Fame duo of guard John Stockton and forward Karl Malone.

9 **Seattle SuperSonics (2001–02 to '07–08)**

Before his blue-and-orange Number 35 jersey became a favorite among NBA fans, superstar Kevin Durant wore green and gold for the Seattle SuperSonics. The Sonics moved to Oklahoma City after the '07–08 season, but their uniforms remain a retro favorite.

10 **Cleveland Cavaliers (1994–95 to '98–99)**

The Cavs have made many color changes over the franchise's history: from dark red and gold to orange and royal blue to their pastel blue and black mid-'90s look. The jagged blue stripe across the middle of the jersey and shorts was a signature look for the team, even if it didn't last into the next decade.

TOP TEN GREATEST DUOS

1

Michael Jordan and Scottie Pippen

For their 10 seasons together, these two were without question the best in NBA history. They were a handful on offense, Jordan becoming the most unstoppable 1-on-1 player ever and Pippen a versatile scoring and playmaking threat. They were even tougher on defense, which is a big reason why they won six NBA titles together, each coming in their last six full seasons together.

2 Kobe Bryant and Shaquille O'Neal

Bryant and O'Neal formed the best inside-outside combination the league has ever seen. Shaq was simply unstoppable on the low block and dominant on the defensive end as well. Bryant, just coming into his prime during their time together, became the league's most dangerous shot-maker inside the three-point arc. The duo led L.A. to a three-peat from 1999–2000 to 2001–02.

3 Larry Bird and Kevin McHale

Bird (*left*) and McHale were incredibly skilled forwards. Bird was a do-it-all superstar, running the show for the Celtics in the 1980s. McHale was a savvy low-post scoring threat. Along with center Robert Parish, they formed the greatest frontcourt in NBA history. Boston went to five NBA Finals and won three titles with these two leading the way.

4 John Stockton and Karl Malone

The pick-and-roll is the greatest play in basketball, and no one ran it better than this Utah Jazz duo. Stockton (*sitting*) was the heady point guard with an uncanny feel for keeping opponents off-balance. Malone was the burly power forward who was too explosive to contain. Stockton is the NBA's all time assists leader, while Malone is second all time in points.

7 Oscar Robertson and Kareem Abdul-Jabbar

These two played four seasons together in Milwaukee, and they were the final years of Robertson's career. The versatility of Robertson (*right*) on the perimeter, along with Kareem's dominance in the paint, was enough to lift the Bucks to the only title in team history, in 1970–71. Milwaukee posted a .756 regular-season win percentage during this duo's time together.

8 Bill Russell and Bob Cousy

With Cousy (*left*) running the point and Russell patrolling the paint, the Boston Celtics of the 1950s and '60s were the greatest dynasty in basketball history. Russell and Cousy played seven seasons together, and Boston won the NBA title in six of those years (they lost in the Finals the other year). They combined to win five NBA MVP awards during that seven-year run.

9 Isiah Thomas and Joe Dumars

The Detroit Pistons of the 1980s were known as the "Bad Boys" due to their physical style of play. Leading the way was two of their little guys: Thomas (*right*) and Dumars. Thomas was the playmaker, running the offense and often taking over in big games. Dumars was a sharpshooter and a lockdown defender. Together, they led Detroit to back-to-back titles in 1988–89 and '89–90.

5 Magic Johnson and Kareem Abdul-Jabbar

The stars of the "Showtime" Lakers of the 1980s, these two were dominant and dazzling. Johnson (*right*) was a 6'9" point guard with incredible court vision and a knack for delivering in big games. Abdul-Jabbar was unstoppable, capable of powering through opponents or using his patented skyhook to score over them. The two won five titles together in L.A.

10 Walt Frazier and Willis Reed

The New York Knicks have won two titles. They both came courtesy of Frazier (*left*) and Reed, one of the NBA's best-ever guard–center tandems. A smooth playmaker, Frazier's game meshed perfectly with Reed's skills in the low post and midrange. The two brought New York to the Finals three times during their seven seasons together.

6 LeBron James and Dwyane Wade

James (*left*) nearly lifted a sorry Cleveland Cavaliers franchise to the promised land. But it wasn't until he teamed up with D-Wade that The King started to get his rings. They won two titles in their first three seasons together, and more should be on the way. LeBron's best skill is his ability to create for teammates, and in Wade he has a fellow superstar who can take full advantage of those playmaking skills. Add in their superior and versatile defensive skills, and you have an all-time great pairing.

1 **Boston Celtics receive draft rights to Bill Russell / St. Louis Hawks receive Ed Macauley and draft rights to Cliff Hagan**

Celtics coach Red Auerbach was desperate to get Russell, believing the big man from the University of San Francisco was the missing piece on his Celtics team. But Boston was selecting too low in the 1956 draft to get their man. The Hawks drafted Russell second overall, and convinced Auerbach to part with Macauley, a star and a St. Louis native, and the promising Hagan. In a way, the trade worked for both sides. All three players are Hall of Famers, and the two teams met in the Finals in four of the next five seasons. Boston won four of those match-ups, and Russell was the main reason. He played a big role in helping to launch a dynasty that won an amazing 11 titles in 13 years.

2 **Los Angeles Lakers receive Kareem Abdul-Jabbar and Walt Wesley / Milwaukee Bucks receive Elmore Smith, Brian Winters, Dave Meyers, and Junior Bridgeman**

The Bucks really had no choice but to trade their superstar center. While he had won a title in Milwaukee and said he liked the fans, the Brooklyn native didn't feel he fit with the culture of the city. So after the 1974–75 season, he demanded a trade to either New York or Los Angeles. The Bucks did what they could, acquiring quality players in Smith and Winters, and promising youngsters in Meyers and Bridgeman (though neither panned out). But Abdul-Jabbar was a game-changer in L.A. He won five titles and three MVP awards playing with the Lakers, and finished his career as the NBA's all-time leading scorer.

3 **Milwaukee Bucks receive Oscar Robertson / Cincinnati Royals receive Flynn Robinson and Charlie Paulk**

This trade, made before the 1970–71 season, was a stunner. Robertson had spent a decade as one of the NBA's best all-around players for the Royals, and Cincinnati was the same city in which he was a collegiate superstar. There were rumors that Royals coach Bob Cousy didn't like sharing the spotlight with a man who had broken many of Cousy's records. The Bucks were more than happy to take "The Big O." In his first season in Milwaukee, he teamed with young big man Lew Alcindor (who changed his name to Kareem Abdul-Jabbar after the season) to win an NBA title. For the Royals, Robinson was a decent player, while Paulk bounced around and had little success in the league.

4 **Boston Celtics receive Kevin Garnett / Minnesota Timberwolves receive Al Jefferson, Ryan Gomes, Sebastian Telfair, Gerald Green, Theo Ratliff, and two first-round picks**

The once-proud Celtics had fallen on hard times, going 24–58 in 2006–07. Garnett had fallen on hard times, too. With a weak supporting cast in Minnesota he was never on a true contender. Boston made two huge moves that offseason, acquiring Garnett as well as getting Ray Allen from the Seattle SuperSonics. Those two stars joined Paul Pierce to bring a title back to Boston in '07–08, the first for all three players. The Timberwolves had received a few offers for Garnett, and they clearly chose the wrong one. Of the players and picks they received (seven combined, the most ever in a trade for one player), only Jefferson became an impact player.

5 **Boston Celtics receive Robert Parish and 3rd overall pick of 1980 draft / Golden State Warriors receive the 1st and 13th picks of the 1980 draft**

The previous offseason, the Celtics had signed free agent forward M.L. Carr, and under NBA rules they had to compensate the Detroit Pistons. So they traded star forward Bob McAdoo for two first-round picks from Detroit. When the Pistons went 16–66 in 1979–80, one of those picks became Number 1 overall. They traded both picks from Detroit to Golden State for Parish, who became a Hall of Famer. The pick they got from the Warriors was used on Kevin McHale, another future Hall of Famer. Meanwhile, the Warriors drafted Joe Barry Carroll first overall. He turned out to be a solid player, but nowhere near Parish or McHale talent-wise.

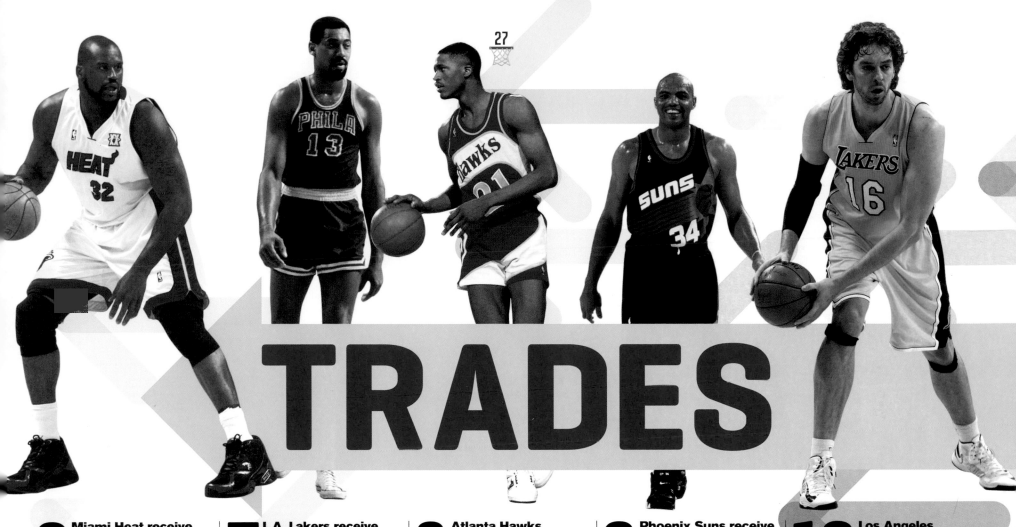

TRADES

6 **Miami Heat receive Shaquille O'Neal / Los Angeles Lakers receive Caron Butler, Lamar Odom, Brian Grant, and a first-round draft pick**

The Lakers had won three titles with Shaq leading the way. And when they acquired veteran stars Karl Malone and Gary Payton to play alongside Shaq and Kobe Bryant in 2003–04, they seemed destined for a fourth. But the team collapsed in the NBA Finals, losing to the underdog Detroit Pistons in five games. Shaq reportedly wasn't getting along with Kobe, legendary head coach Phil Jackson was leaving, and O'Neal felt he deserved a raise. Instead, he was traded to Miami for a package of good, but not great, players. Two years later, Shaq and Dwyane Wade brought Miami its first title. The Lakers, on the other hand, missed the playoffs the following season.

7 **L.A. Lakers receive Wilt Chamberlain / Philadelphia 76ers receive Darrall Imhoff, Jerry Chambers, and Archie Clark**

In 1967–68, Chamberlain won his third consecutive MVP award. Head coach Alex Hannum left after the season, and according to general manager Jack Ramsey, Chamberlain originally asked to become the Sixers' player-coach. But when Chamberlain returned from a trip to the West Coast later that offseason, he had a change of heart: He demanded to be traded out west. Ramsey worked out a deal with the Lakers, bringing back Imhoff, a solid center, a promising young guard in Clark, and Chambers, who was traded to Phoenix in the same offseason. The 32-year-old Chamberlain wasn't as dominant as he was earlier in his career, but he did help L.A. to a title in 1972.

8 **Atlanta Hawks receive Dominique Wilkins / Utah Jazz receive John Drew, Freeman Williams, and cash**

The Jazz were struggling financially during the 1982 offseason, but that was still no excuse for making one of the most lopsided trades in NBA history. They had drafted Wilkins, a collegiate star at the University of Georgia, third overall in the '82 draft. But Wilkins didn't want to play in Utah, and the Jazz found they couldn't afford him. The Hawks were more than happy to take the hometown hero off the Jazz's hands. Drew and Williams were proven veterans. But Williams played only 18 games in a Jazz uniform. Drew was solid, and he helped lead the Jazz to their first playoff berth, but he played only three seasons in Utah. Meanwhile, Wilkins was one of the league's best, and most exciting, scorers in the 1980s.

9 **Phoenix Suns receive Charles Barkley / Philadelphia 76ers receive Jeff Hornacek, Tim Perry, and Andrew Lang**

Barkley was one of the NBA's most popular stars. But with the 76ers struggling to build a team that could compete with the mighty Chicago Bulls, he wanted a change of scenery. He got it in Phoenix before the 1992–93 season. The arrival of Barkley injected new life in Phoenix, as the Suns won the Western Conference title. Unfortunately, Michael Jordan and the Bulls were waiting for them in the Finals. Barkley had a huge series, including a triple-double in a heartbreaking Game 4 loss in Chicago, but the Suns lost in six games. Barkley never got back to the Finals. Despite solid play from Hornacek, Philly struggled without Barkley. They didn't make the playoffs again until Allen Iverson led them there in '98–99.

10 **Los Angeles Lakers receive Pau Gasol and a second-round draft pick / Memphis Grizzlies receive Kwame Brown, Javaris Crittenton, Aaron McKie, the draft rights to Marc Gasol, and two first-round draft picks**

After the Lakers traded Shaquille O'Neal following the 2003–04 season, they didn't get back on top until they acquired Pau Gasol from Memphis at the '07–08 midseason trade deadline. The Lakers went to the NBA Finals in each of the first three postseasons Kobe Bryant and Gasol played together, winning back-to-back titles in '08–09 and '09–10. None of the veterans Memphis received were of any value. But they ended up with a gem in Marc Gasol, a former second-round pick playing overseas, and Pau's little brother. Marc become a star for the rebuilt Grizzlies.

TOP 10 NBA FINALS GAMES

1 Spurs vs. Heat: 2013, Game 6

The defending champion Miami Heat were on the brink of elimination on their home court. They trailed the San Antonio Spurs 3–2 in the series, and were down 10 entering the fourth quarter. The Heat stormed back, but San Antonio led by five with less than 30 seconds left. That's when LeBron James hit a three-pointer. Kawhi Leonard made only one of two free throws on the Spurs' next possession, making it a three-point game and giving the Heat one last chance. James missed a three-pointer, but Chris Bosh got the rebound and passed it to the corner to Ray Allen, who calmly knocked down the shot with five seconds left, forcing overtime. The Heat went on to win, and took Game 7 as well, for their second consecutive title.

2 Jazz vs. Bulls
1997, Game 5

With the Finals tied, 2–2, the Chicago Bulls were looking to steal a game in Utah. The problem, however, was that superstar Michael Jordan had become ill with a stomach bug the afternoon of the game. Though he was very sick, Jordan still shined. With less than a minute left and the Jazz protecting an 85–84 lead, Jordan hit the first of two free throws to tie it, but missed the second. The rebound was tipped and eventually ended up back in Jordan's hands. He re-set the offense, and when Scottie Pippen drew a double-team, he kicked it back to MJ, who buried a three-pointer. The lasting image of the "flu game" is Pippen holding up an exhausted Jordan (see page 86), who finished the night with 38 points in a 90–88 Bulls win.

3 Suns vs. Celtics
1976, Game 5

This finals game featured plenty of controversy. At the end of the first overtime, officials ignored Boston's Paul Silas as he signaled for a timeout. The Celtics had none left, and should have been given a technical. At the end of the second overtime, John Havlicek put the Celtics up 111–110. The shot went through with two seconds left, but the clock didn't stop. Fans stormed the court, but the refs put one second back. Though they had no timeouts left, the Suns asked for one anyway. They were assessed a technical, and Boston went up two. It was a good move for the Suns, who moved the ball up to midcourt for the inbounds play. Gar Heard took the inbounds pass and hit a jumper to beat the buzzer, forcing a third overtime. With numerous players fouled out, Boston turned to Glenn McDonald in the third overtime. He delivered six points, and the Celtics came away with a 128–126 win.

5 Lakers vs. Celtics
1962, Game 7

This series marked the first time the Celtics and Lakers had met in the NBA Finals since the Lakers relocated from Minneapolis to Los Angeles. And the deciding game was a classic. Elgin Baylor was unstoppable for the Lakers, finishing with 41 points, while Jerry West added 35. The Celtics led 100–96 late, but L.A.'s Frank Selvy scored on back-to-back fastbreak lay-ups to tie it. Selvy had a chance to win it at the buzzer, but he missed a baseline jump shot. Boston's Bill Russell grabbed the rebound, one of 40 he grabbed that game, sending it to overtime. Boston controlled the extra period behind Russell, Sam Jones, and Frank Ramsey, and held on for a 110–107 victory. It would be the end of the first chapter in the storied Boston–L.A. rivalry.

4 Hawks vs. Celtics
1957, Game 7

The Boston Celtics and St. Louis Hawks played a roller coaster of a game to decide the NBA champion. The teams traded leads in the final minute of regulation, with legends like Bill Russell of the Celtics, then a rookie, and the Hawks' Bob Pettit making big plays down the stretch. Pettit's two late free throws forced overtime. The Celtics led 113–111 with time winding down when Jack Coleman knocked down a jump shot to force a second OT. Jim Loscutoff made two free throws late to give the Celtics a 125–123 lead with just seconds left. With the team in foul trouble, St. Louis player-coach Alex Hannum stepped onto the court for the first time in the series. His plan was to throw the ball the length of the court off the backboard, hoping that Pettit would grab it for an open shot. The pass worked, but Pettit missed the shot. The Celtics won their first title in franchise history.

6 Celtics vs. Lakers
2010, Game 7

Of all the games in the storied Boston Celtics–Los Angeles Lakers rivalry, this might have been the hardest-fought. Both teams played with an incredible tenacity on defense. Lakers star Kobe Bryant was held to 23 points on 6-of-24 shooting from the field. On Boston's side, Paul Pierce had just 18 points on 5-for-15 shooting, while sharpshooter Ray Allen was 3-for-14, finishing with 13 points. The teams scrapped for every point, and the lead rarely became more than three points for either team during the fourth quarter. In the final six minutes, clutch free throw shooting from Bryant and Pau Gasol, a key three-pointer from Ron Artest, and two final free throws from reserve guard Sasha Vujacic cemented the win for L.A., 83–79. The win gave the Lakers a second straight NBA title.

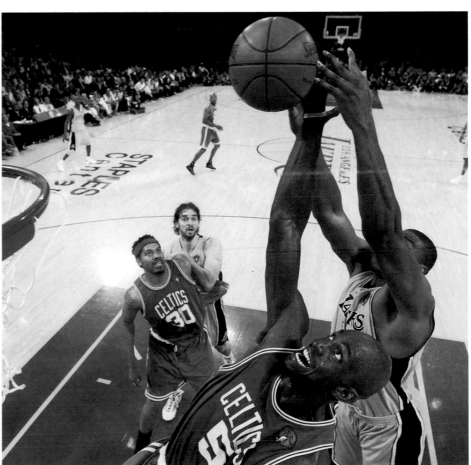

7 Lakers vs. Knicks
1970, Game 3

With the New York Knicks and Los Angeles Lakers tied at one game apiece, the stage was set for one of the most dramatic finishes in Finals history. Dave DeBusschere made a jumper with three seconds left to give the Knicks a 102–100 lead. The Lakers were seemingly finished. Wilt Chamberlain inbounded to Jerry West who took a couple of dribbles and heaved up a 60-foot shot from beyond half court. And it went in. Despite the game-tying shot from "Mr. Clutch" (there were no three-pointers in 1970, so the long shot counted for only two), the Lakers didn't carry much momentum into overtime. The Knicks ended up hanging on for a 111–108 win.

9 Mavericks vs. Heat
2011, Game 2

The Dallas Mavericks were in a lot of trouble. Already considered an underdog against the Miami Heat and their newly formed Big Three — LeBron James, Dwyane Wade, and Chris Bosh — the Mavs trailed 1–0 in the series and were down 15 points with less than seven minutes to go in Game 2. On top of that, star forward Dirk Nowitzki had a torn tendon in his left middle finger. But somehow, the Mavs rallied. Nowitzki's basket with just under a minute to go tied the game at 90. He made a three-pointer 30 seconds later to give Dallas the lead, but Heat guard Mario Chalmers matched the shot at the other end with 25 seconds left. But there was no denying Dirk. Isolated against Bosh, he drove left and made the game winning layup with just 3.6 seconds remaining. The Mavs took the game, and eventually the series, for the franchise's first title.

8 76ers vs. Lakers
2001, Game 1

Behind Shaquille O'Neal and Kobe Bryant, the Los Angeles Lakers were an unstoppable juggernaut entering the 2001 Finals. They swept their first three postseason opponents, and dating back to the regular season had a 19-game winning streak. Playing the underdog Philadelphia 76ers at home, the Lakers figured to have no problems in Game 1. Sixers star Allen Iverson had other ideas. Behind their superstar guard, Philly opened up a 15-point lead in the third quarter. The Lakers turned up the heat defensively, using 6-foot guard Tyronn Lue to guard the 6-foot Iverson, and eventually forced overtime. After L.A. scored the first five points in OT, Iverson brought Philly back. His three-pointer over Lue gave them the lead for good, and the Sixers finished off the upset, 107–101, behind A.I.'s 48 points. It was a major shocker, but it was also a wake-up call for L.A. The Lakers won the next four games to take the NBA title.

10 Celtics vs. Lakers
1969, Game 7

Los Angeles Lakers owner Jack Kent Cooke was confident that his team would beat the Boston Celtics in Game 7. So much so that he had already arranged balloons and a championship banner in the rafters, and he left a flyer on every seat in The Forum guaranteeing the win. The Celtics had seen the flyers. During pre-game warmups, Celtics player-coach Bill Russell spotted the balloons and had a message for rival Jerry West: Those balloons are staying up there. The Celtics controlled the action for most of the game, taking a 15-point lead into the fourth quarter. L.A. made it interesting, getting to within one point of the Celtics with less than two minutes left. Boston's Don Nelson got a friendly bounce on a desperation jump shot to stretch the lead to three, and the Celtics held on for a 108–106 victory, giving Russell his 11th career title. West finished the game with a triple-double (42 points, 13 rebounds, 12 assists) and was named Finals MVP. He remains the only player from a losing team to win the award.

1 Lisa Leslie

Leslie was the most dominant post player in WNBA history. The 6'5" center had an unmatched combination of quickness, power, and grace. She was a three-time MVP and led the Los Angeles Sparks to two titles. She also helped usher in women's basketball's new breed of athletic players; Leslie was the first player to dunk in a WNBA game. She ranks in the top five in career points, rebounds, and blocks.

2 Cynthia Cooper

When the WNBA started play in 1997, Cooper was the league's dominant player. Coming off a strong pro career overseas, she was 34 when she joined the Houston Comets. Cooper was an elite scorer and a crafty playmaker, winning MVP in each of the WNBA's first two seasons, the scoring title in each of the first three, and Finals MVP honors in each of the first four, her only four full seasons in the league.

TOP IO WNE

5 Candace Parker

When the Los Angeles Sparks drafted the ultra-athletic 6'4" center first overall in 2008, many considered Parker to be the greatest talent ever to come into the league. She lived up to the hype right away, becoming the only rookie in league history to win MVP honors. In 2013, she became only the fifth two-time WNBA MVP. Through '13, Parker had led the league in rebounding three times and shot-blocking twice.

6 Diana Taurasi

Taurasi is the greatest pure scorer the women's game has ever seen. At 6'0" with the athleticism, ball-handling skills, and body control to create shots anywhere on the court, she's the only WNBA player to average 24 or more points per game in a season. And she did it twice (2006 and '08). The league's only five-time scoring champion, Taurasi was WNBA MVP in 2009, and has led the Phoenix Mercury to two titles.

7 Tamika Catchings

The Indiana Fever forward has the skills of a guard. She's an elite shooter and, at 6'1", has the size to get her shot off against anyone. By the end of 2013, she was third on the WNBA's all-time scoring and rebounding lists. As good as she is on offense, it's tenacious defense that makes her great. Catchings is the league's only five-time Defensive Player of the Year, and has more steals than anyone in WNBA history.

3 Lauren Jackson

A teenage superstar in her native Australia during the 1990s, the 6'5" Jackson is a skilled and tough-as-nails center. The Seattle Storm made her the top pick of the 2001 draft, and in her third season she won her first of three scoring titles. The first international player to win league MVP honors, Jackson has led Seattle to two WNBA titles (2004, '10). In 2010, she became the league's third three-time MVP.

4 Sheryl Swoopes

Swoopes is the greatest two-way player in league history. Along with two scoring titles, her combination of size (6'0"), quickness, and toughness made her an elite defensive player. She won three Defensive Player of the Year awards to go along with her three MVPs. The four-time WNBA champion was a game-changer off the court, too. Nike's "Air Swoopes" was the first signature shoe for a WNBA player.

A PLAYERS

8 Tina Thompson

Thompson was the first overall pick of the WNBA's first collegiate draft, in 1997. She played 17 seasons and 496 games, more than any other player in league history. Thompson was a key piece of a Houston Comets team that won titles in each of the WNBA's first four years of existence. The power forward was a nine-time All-Star and retired after 2013 as the league's all-time leading scorer (7,488 points).

9 Cappie Pondexter

The cat-quick point guard is an electrifying offensive force. At just 5'9", Pondexter uses quickness, toughness, and creative ball-handling to drive through defenses. In her first postseason, 2007, she averaged 23.9 points and won Finals MVP honors — she won her first of two WNBA titles with the Phoenix Mercury. Through the 2013 season, she was second in career scoring average among active players (19.2).

10 Sue Bird

As good as Lauren Jackson has been throughout her career, the Seattle Storm wouldn't have become one of the WNBA's elite franchises without Bird. The point guard's rookie year was the first time the Storm ever made the playoffs, and Bird has teamed up with Jackson to bring two titles to Seattle. A floor general with outstanding court vision, the seven-time All-Star is also one of the league's top sharpshooters.

TOP 10 QUOTES

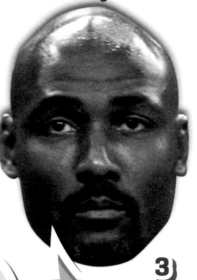

1

"Which one of you is going to come in second?"

-Larry Bird-

2

"We all get heavier as we get older because there's a lot more information in our heads. Our heads weigh more."

-Vlade Divac-

3

"What excites me the most is when a coach calls a timeout and chews out his forward because I just dunked on his head."

-Karl Malone-

4

"We are in the business of kicking butt, and business is very, very good."

-Charles Barkley-

5

"Don't ever underestimate the heart of a champion."

-Rudy Tomjanovich-

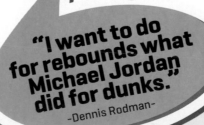

6

"I'm like the Pythagorean theorem. Not too many people know the answer to my game."

-Shaquille O'Neal-

7

"Nobody roots for Goliath."

-Wilt Chamberlain-

8

"I want to do for rebounds what Michael Jordan did for dunks."

-Dennis Rodman-

9

"I'm gonna take my talents to South Beach and join the Miami Heat."

-LeBron James-

10

"Talent wins games, but teamwork and intelligence win championships."

-Michael Jordan-

Top 10 Sneakers

1 **Air Jordan XI**
This is the iconic shoe worn by Michael Jordan in the movie *Space Jam*. It looks great both on and off the court, and that versatility alone is enough to make this our pick for the best basketball sneaker of all time.

2 **Air Jordan III**
The Air Jordan III is similar to the earlier versions of the Jordan sneakers, but this one had a little something different: a unique pattern in the leather. These were also the first sneakers to include the famous "Jumpman" logo.

3 **Air Force I**
The first sneaker to feature Nike Air cushioning, the Air Force I became one of the best-known shoes in history. It's named after the aircraft that carries the President of the United States, the Air Force One.

4 **Nike Air Zoom Huarache 2k4**
Worn by seemingly every player in the NBA and college when it was first released, these performed well and included design elements of past Nike shoes. "Huarache" is a Spanish word for a leather sandal.

5 **Converse Chuck Taylor All-Stars**
Named after basketball player and Converse salesman Chuck Taylor, this was the first iconic sneaker in basketball history. The canvas shoes were wildly popular throughout the 1970s.

6 **Reebok Pump**
These featured a basketball-shaped button on the tongue that pumped air into the cushioning. Boston Celtics guard Dee Brown famously stopped to "pump" his shoes before his best dunk during the 1991 Slam Dunk Contest.

7 **Air Jordan I**
The sneaker that started it all is also one of the nicest-looking sneakers to ever hit the court. The Jordan collection started with a bang and never looked back. The Air Jordan 1 has been released more than any other model of Air Jordans.

8 **Air Penny II**
Orlando Magic star Penny Hardaway had an extremely cool logo. This signature shoe came in black-and-white, with blue to represent the Magic. The air bubble on the heel was the icing on the cake for this classic.

9 **Adidas Crazy 8**
Featuring a zig-zag of different colors on the bottom, this shoe is packed with creativity. Numerous stars, including Derrick Rose, have worn these on the court. The one shown here was worn by L.A. Lakers star Kobe Bryant.

10 **Reebok Answer IV**
A mid-cut sneaker featuring a zipper and a blend of colors running from the tongue to the heel, this signature shoe of Philadelphia 76ers superstar Allen Iverson was unlike any other.

TOP 10 GAME WINNING SHOTS

1 Michael Jordan
May 7, 1989

It was Game 5 of a best-of-five first-round playoff series between the underdog Chicago Bulls and the Cleveland Cavaliers. The Bulls trailed, 100–99, but had the ball for one last shot. On the inbounds pass, the Cavs double-teamed Jordan, but he shook free anyway. Jordan took two dribbles to the foul line with defensive ace Craig Ehlo shadowing him. He had to double-clutch as Ehlo flew by, but the series-clinching shot rattled in anyway. It was a young Jordan's first truly legendary NBA moment.

3 Michael Jordan (June 14, 1998)
The Chicago Bulls led the NBA Finals series, 3–2, but trailed by one late in Game 6. Jordan stole the ball from Utah Jazz star Karl Malone. Guarded by Bryon Russell, he pulled up near the top of the key as Russell lost his footing. The shot was perfect, clinching Jordan's sixth title.

4 Magic Johnson (June 9, 1987)
The Los Angeles Lakers trailed the Boston Celtics, 106–105, with seven seconds left in Game 4 of the NBA Finals. Johnson got the ball on the left wing with Kevin McHale guarding him. Magic drove across the lane against the bigger defender and nailed a running hook shot to win it.

5 Dennis Johnson (May 26, 1987)
The Detroit Pistons had the ball and a one-point lead with five seconds left in Game 5 of the Eastern Conference Finals. That's when Boston's Larry Bird stole an inbounds pass. Falling out of bounds on the baseline, he shoveled a pass to Johnson. D.J. laid it in, and Boston stole the win.

6 Kobe Bryant (April 30, 2006)
Bryant's last-second shot had forced overtime in Game 4 of a first-round playoff series against the Phoenix Suns. With L.A. trailing by one late in OT, he dribbled to the right wing and pulled up for a jumper over two defenders. It went through the net as the buzzer sounded.

2 Derek Fisher
May 13, 2004

In a key Game 5 of a second-round playoff series, Tim Duncan's long fadeaway jumper had given the San Antonio Spurs a 73–72 lead with just 0.4 seconds left. All the Lakers could do was throw up a prayer. With his back to the basket, Fisher caught the inbounds pass on the left wing and heaved a shot as he spun around. His prayer was answered; nothing but net.

7 Damian Lillard (May 2, 2014)

The Houston Rockets scored with just 0.9 seconds remaining to take a 98–96 lead over the Portland Trail Blazers in Game 6 of a first-round playoff series. It set the stage for Lillard's miraculous buzzer-beating three-pointer, which closed out the series for Portland.

8 Robert Horry (May 26, 2002)

Down two in the final seconds of Game 4 in the Western Conference Finals, L.A. needed a big shot. Stars Kobe Bryant and Shaquille O'Neal missed from close range, but the rebound got knocked outside to Horry. "Big Shot Bob" calmly knocked down a three-pointer to win it.

9 Ralph Sampson (May 21, 1986)

Houston was on the verge of toppling the Lakers in the Western Conference Finals. With Game 5 tied, 112–112, and one second left, Sampson caught the inbounds pass with his back to the basket, twisted and flipped a shot over his head. It bounced off the front rim then fell through.

10 Ron Artest (May 27, 2010)

Tied with the Phoenix Suns in Game 5 of the Western Conference Finals, Lakers star Kobe Bryant's last-second shot was short. But teammate Ron Artest (Number 37) was in the right place. He caught the air ball, and flipped it in off the backboard at the buzzer.

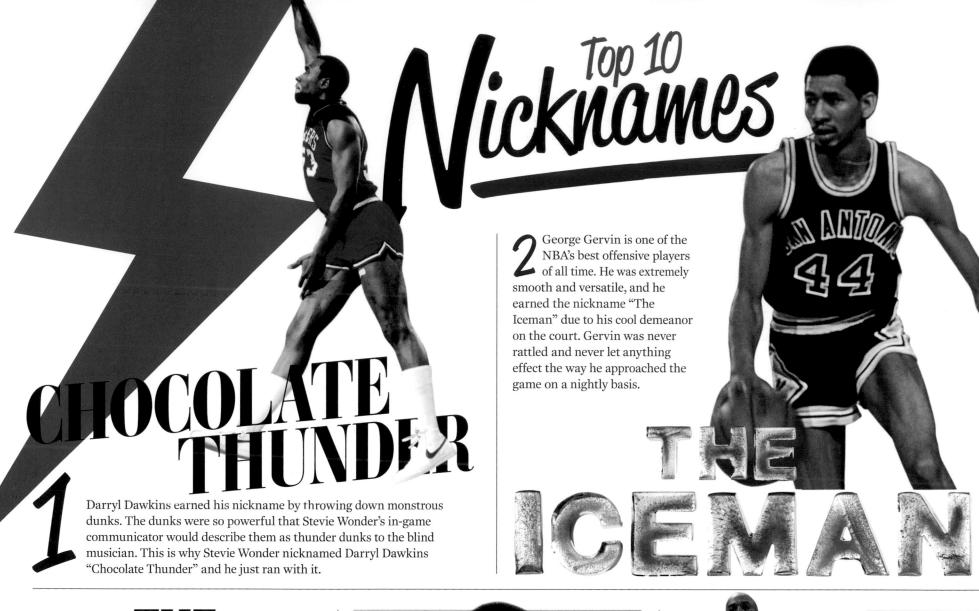

Top 10 Nicknames

2
George Gervin is one of the NBA's best offensive players of all time. He was extremely smooth and versatile, and he earned the nickname "The Iceman" due to his cool demeanor on the court. Gervin was never rattled and never let anything effect the way he approached the game on a nightly basis.

CHOCOLATE THUNDER

1
Darryl Dawkins earned his nickname by throwing down monstrous dunks. The dunks were so powerful that Stevie Wonder's in-game communicator would describe them as thunder dunks to the blind musician. This is why Stevie Wonder nicknamed Darryl Dawkins "Chocolate Thunder" and he just ran with it.

THE ICEMAN

—THE— TRUTH

5
When Paul Pierce was just 23 years old, he played a strong game against Shaquille O'Neal and the Los Angeles Lakers. Shaq was impressed with the way Pierce performed, and after the game he kept saying that Paul Pierce was "the truth." This would eventually stick as a nickname for the 10-time All-Star and 2008 Finals MVP.

Dr. J

6
Julius Erving was a remarkably talented basketball player — he played at a high level in both the ABA and NBA. Erving got his nickname in high school, where one of his teammates started to call him "the doctor." That name evolved into "Dr. J" — it remains one of the most famous nicknames in basketball history.

THE GLOVE

7
Gary Payton is a nine-time All-Star and two-time All-NBA First Teamer. The point guard was at his best in the 13 years he played for the Seattle SuperSonics. Payton is one of the best defenders in NBA history. He was the 1996 NBA Defensive Player of the Year and his ability to stick close to his opponents earned him the nickname, "The Glove."

THE MAILMAN

3 Karl Malone is one of the most productive players in NBA history. In his 19 seasons in the NBA, Malone averaged 25.0 PPG and 10.1 RPG. He never had a season in which he averaged less than 13.2 PPG. Malone's consistency earned him the nickname "The Mailman." This was given to the forward because no matter what the circumstances were, the big man always delivered outstanding performances.

The Big O

4 Oscar Robertson was an exceptional player who had an amazing resume as an NBA player. Robertson was the 1964 league MVP and was an NBA champion in 1971. He was a unique player due to his size. As a 6' 5" point guard, he was massive for his position at the time. That's what earned him the nickname, "The Big O."

THE DREAM

8 Hakeem Olajuwon was one of a kind in terms of his play as a center for the Houston Rockets. Olajuwon had the best footwork in NBA history for a big man and he even earned the nickname, "The Dream," due to his grace on and off the court. His signature move would even be called "The Dream Shake."

Pistol Pete

9 Pete Maravich averaged more than 40 points per game three straight college seasons at LSU. The guard was a magician with the ball and he was a gunner from deep. With his shooting ability, Maravich often shot the ball fluidly off the dribble. He had a quick trigger, and that was why he earned the nickname "Pistol Pete."

THE ANSWER

10 Allen Iverson worked extremely hard on the basketball court. As a member of the Philadelphia 76ers, he had to because of the lack of talent on the rest of the team. When Iverson was drafted by the Sixers, they had hoped he would turn around the franchise. Iverson was "the answer" to their problems, and he had a tattoo with the nickname to show for it.

Top 10 Mascots

1

Benny the Bull

Benny has been entertaining Bulls fans for more than 40 years. In 2013, a survey of fans ranked mascots across all sports based on categories such as likeability, photo-friendliness, interaction, and fun. Benny was ranked Number 1.

2
Go the Gorilla
It's pretty funny when a mascot has nothing to do with a team's name. Go is not only a wacky choice to represent the Phoenix Suns, but he's an impressive athlete as well. Few mascots can match his acrobatic dunks off the trampoline.

3
Rumble the Bison
Replacing the beloved Squatch after the Seattle SuperSonics moved to Oklahoma City was a tall task, but Rumble has been up to it. He debuted midseason in 2008–09, and was named the NBA's Mascot of the Year at the league mascot meetings just six months later.

4
Rocky the Mountain Lion
Known best for his backward halfcourt shot at Denver Nuggets games, Rocky is one of the NBA's most beloved mascots. He won the award for Most Awesome Mascot at the Cartoon Network's Hall of Game Awards in 2013.

5
Bango
Bango is considered to be a legend among NBA mascots. The Milwaukee Bucks mascot once climbed atop a 20-foot ladder and did a backflip dunk. With stunts like that, it's no wonder the deer once suffered a torn ACL.

6
Squatch
The SuperSonics' mascot once tried to jump 30 cars on inline skates. He also inspired a song by the rock band Presidents of the United States of America. Squatch's whereabouts have remained a mystery ever since the Sonics relocated to Oklahoma City.

7

Hugo the Hornet

The cuddly Hugo has an alter ego: Super Hugo. A sleek dunking machine, Super Hugo won three NBA Mascot Slam Dunk Championships. It was announced in late 2013 that Hugo would return in 2014–15 with the Charlotte Bobcats becoming the Charlotte Hornets.

8

Grizz

Grizz has been cheering on the Grizzlies since the mid-1990s, when the team was still in Vancouver. He was named NBA's Mascot of the Year in 2011 and is one mascot you don't want to mess with. He is known to sometimes wear a mask and cape to change into his alter ego, Super Grizz. During a break in the action in a February 2014 game, Super Grizz lifted a fan of the opposing Washington Wizards before slamming him through a table to complete a popular wrestling move called a powerbomb (okay, okay, it was just an act).

9

G-Man

The muscle-bound mascot helped Washington Wizards star John Wall win the 2014 Slam Dunk Contest. G-Man stood next to the basket and held a ball over his head. While leaping over him, Wall grabbed the ball and then slammed home a reverse dunk.

10

Harry The Hawk

The Atlanta Hawks hatched Harry in 1985, and he has been thrilling Atlanta fans ever since with his dancing, stair-sledding, and stilt-walking. The team claims they drafted him instead of former Boston Celtics legend Larry *Bird*.

DRAFT STEALS

1 Manu Ginobili
1999, 2nd round, 57th overall, San Antonio Spurs

Many NBA teams these days use late second-round picks to select overseas prospects that they hope will develop more before coming to the NBA. The strategy paid off in a big way for the Spurs when they took Ginobili, an Argentine guard playing in Italy, with the second-to-last pick of the 1999 draft. Ginobili stayed in Spain for three more seasons after he was drafted. Since joining the Spurs, he has developed into an All-Star, a top sixth man, and a key player on three of San Antonio's championship teams.

2 Alex English
1976, 2nd round, 23rd overall, Milwaukee Bucks

A solid but unspectacular player at the University of South Carolina, English was largely overlooked in a deep and talented '76 draft. The Bucks, rebuilding at the time, used him sparingly off the bench in his first two seasons. His career didn't take off until two teams later, when he joined the Denver Nuggets. An efficient scorer who rarely spoke publicly, English averaged 20 points or more in each of his first 10 seasons with Denver, including a scoring title in 1982–83. The eight-time All-Star is now in the Hall of Fame.

3 Dennis Johnson
1976, 2nd round, 29th overall, Seattle SuperSonics

Johnson was a benchwarmer at Dominguez High School in Los Angeles and had taken a job as a forklift operator after graduation. A growth spurt led to interest from a local junior college, and then Pepperdine University. Johnson was considered a great defender but also a troublemaker, causing him to slide down the board. His defense and floor leadership made him an All-Star in Seattle, and he led the Sonics to a title, winning MVP of the '79 Finals. He went on to win two more titles with Boston, providing much-needed perimeter D for the Celtics.

4 Dennis Rodman
1986, 2nd round, 27th overall, Detroit Pistons

Coming from an NAIA college, Southeastern Oklahoma State, Rodman might have slipped even further in the draft if he hadn't dominated at the pre-draft Portsmouth Invitational Tournament. He was a relentless worker, especially when it came to rebounding and defense. He ended up helping Detroit to back-to-back titles, and later won three more with the Chicago Bulls. He ended his pro career as a seven-time rebounding champion and a two-time NBA Defensive Player of the Year.

5 Gilbert Arenas
2001, 2nd round, 30th overall, Golden State Warriors

It was never easy to get a good handle on Arenas's game, especially coming into the draft out of the University of Arizona. He was a unique, score-first combo guard who was unpredictable for opponents and teammates. But before injuries derailed his career, there were few players who could fill it up like Agent Zero. His career took off after joining the Washington Wizards, as the three-time All-Star was top seven in the NBA in scoring three straight seasons (2004–05 to '06–07).

6 Rashard Lewis
1998, 2nd round, 32nd overall, Seattle SuperSonics

Lewis was such a highly regarded prospect coming out of high school in Texas that he was invited to the 1998 draft's "green room," reserved for players expected to be picked early. But on that night, teams kept passing on Lewis. By the time the Sonics called his name, the 18-year-old was in tears. His NBA career was much happier. A lanky power forward who could score inside and out, Lewis became one of the league's most dangerous frontcourt scorers. He played in All-Star games as a member of both the SuperSonics and the Orlando Magic.

7 Marc Gasol
2007, 2nd round, 48th overall, Los Angeles Lakers

When Marc Gasol was playing in Spain, he was mostly known as All-Star Pau Gasol's slightly overweight younger brother. The Lakers took a chance on him in the 2007 draft, left him overseas for a season, and then traded his draft rights to the Memphis Grizzlies in exchange for Pau. Marc came to Memphis for the 2008–09 season slimmed down, and immediately delivered on offense. He's one of the best passing big men in the league. He became a franchise player as his defense improved. Gasol was the 2012–13 Defensive Player of the Year.

8 Nate Archibald
1970, 2nd round, 19th overall, Cincinnati Royals

"Tiny" Archibald had a tremendous career at the University of Texas-El Paso, but he still slipped into the second round of the draft. It was almost immediately clear that the Royals (who soon became the Kansas City Kings) had a steal. In his third season, 1972–73, Archibald led the NBA in scoring and assists, the only player in league history to pull off that feat. Later in his career he took over as the floor general for the Boston Celtics. He helped bring the Hall of Fame frontcourt of Larry Bird, Robert Parish, and Kevin McHale their first title.

9 Drazen Petrovic
1986, 3rd round, 60th overall, Portland Blazers

When the Blazers drafted Petrovic, they weren't sure when or even if the European star would come to the NBA. By the time he arrived in Portland for the 1989–90 season, the Blazers already had a couple of star guards in Clyde Drexler and Terry Porter. Petrovic was traded to the New Jersey Nets midway through his second season and became a star. A savvy ball-handler and out-standing shooter, Petrovic was also a tremendous competitor and prolific scorer. Tragically, he died in a car accident after the '92–93 season, just when his career was taking off.

10 Michael Redd
2000, 2nd round, 43rd overall, Milwaukee Bucks

At Ohio State, Redd was a great scorer who led the Buckeyes to the 1999 Final Four. But in part because of a shaky jump shot, he slipped all the way to the middle of the second round in the 2000 draft. He barely played as a rookie, but apparently he had time to improve his shot. Redd was top 10 in three-point percentage each of the next two years. He ended up an All-Star in 2004 and won a gold medal with the star-studded U.S. team in 2008. He finished among the NBA's top 10 in scoring four times.

ELLISON

BROWN

BOWIE

THABEET
34

FERRY
CLEVELAND

★ DRAFT BUSTS ★

MORRISON
CHARLOTTE
35

MILICIC
PISTONS
31

ODEN
BLAZERS
52

MARTIN
blazers
35

OLOWOKANDI

Darko Milicic
(2nd overall pick, 2003, Detroit Pistons)

Despite winning 50 games the previous season, the Detroit Pistons owned the second pick of the 2003 draft, thanks to a trade with the Memphis Grizzlies. Detroit had a choice of one of three collegiate superstars — Syracuse's Carmelo Anthony, Georgia Tech's Chris Bosh, and Marquette's Dwyane Wade — or Milicic, a 7-footer from Serbia with rare skills and athleticism for his size. Detroit went with Milicic, but he was buried deep on the bench for a veteran Pistons team. He never developed, and averaged just six points and four rebounds per game while bouncing around the league over the course of 10 NBA seasons. Anthony, Bosh, and Wade went with the next three picks; all three quickly became NBA All-Stars.

2 Sam Bowie
(2nd overall pick, 1984, Portland Trail Blazers)
The Portland Trail Blazers were in need of a big man heading into the 1984–85 season, and that's why they selected Bowie, the 7' 1" star from the University of Kentucky, ahead of a University of North Carolina shooting guard named Michael Jordan. Bowie had a decent NBA career, but he battled injuries far too often to become more than a middling big man. Meanwhile, Jordan, selected third overall by the Chicago Bulls, became a legend. The Bulls ended up with six championship rings, while the Blazers ended up wondering what could have been.

3 Adam Morrison
(3rd overall pick, 2006, Charlotte Bobcats)
While playing at Gonzaga University, Morrison often drew comparisons to another sweet-shooting small school forward from a relatively small college: Larry Bird. While he certainly filled up the stat sheet for the Zags, Morrison's pro career came nowhere near Larry Legend's. Morrison was overmatched by the athleticism of NBA defenders as a rookie, then tore his ACL before his second season. He made less than 38 percent of his field goal attempts in each of his three NBA seasons. He played his final season in 2009–10 with the Los Angeles Lakers.

4 Greg Oden
(1st overall pick, 2007, Portland Trail Blazers)
The Blazers were burned by their decision to go with size over scoring in the 1984 draft, when they selected Sam Bowie over Michael Jordan. They made a similar mistake in 1972, when they took LaRue Martin instead of Bob McAdoo. History repeated itself in 2007, when Portland had the top pick of the draft. Oden, a former high school phenom and Ohio State star, was considered a can't-miss franchise center. But he struggled with knee problems as a pro, playing just 82 total games for the Blazers. Kevin Durant, the second pick of the '07 draft, has gone on to become a superstar.

5 Michael Olowokandi
(1st overall pick, 1998, Los Angeles Clippers)
In the 1990s, some considered the Clippers franchise to be cursed. But the reality is that they made too many poor decisions, like drafting Olowokandi. The 7-footer from the University of the Pacific was thought to have big-time upside, but he never tapped into it. There was nothing sweet about the Kandi Man's career, which lasted nine seasons. He averaged double-digit points in just two of them. Three players drafted later in Round 1 — Vince Carter, Dirk Nowitzki, and Paul Pierce — have enjoyed outstanding NBA careers.

6 Kwame Brown
(1st overall pick, 2001, Washington Wizards)
There's no denying that Michael Jordan was one of the greatest players of all time. But his career as an NBA executive got off to a rough start. Jordan, who was the Wizards' president of basketball operations in 2001, used the top pick of the draft to select Brown, a high school star from Georgia. "This is a great beginning for this franchise, and it starts with him," Jordan said after selecting Brown. Despite a combination of size (6' 11") and athleticism, Brown averaged only 6.6 points per game over a 12-year career.

7 Danny Ferry
(2nd overall pick, 1989, Los Angeles Clippers)
College basketball's national player of the year in 1988–89, the Duke University star had no interest in playing for the Clippers. After being selected second overall in the '89 draft, Ferry refused to sign with L.A. and instead signed with a team in Italy. One year later, the Clippers traded his rights to the Cleveland Cavaliers. He wasn't worth the wait. The Cavs signed Ferry to a 10-year contract, but he spent most of his time in the league as a middling bench player, averaging 7.0 points per game for his career.

8 LaRue Martin
(1st overall pick, 1972, Portland Trail Blazers)
Martin became something of a legend in college. His team, Loyola-Chicago, hosted an unstoppable UCLA squad in 1972. The Bruins overpowered Loyola, but Martin more than held his own against legendary Bruins big man Bill Walton, putting up 19 points and 18 rebounds. The Blazers were impressed enough that they made Martin the top pick of the '72 draft, but he was never up to the task in the pros. Martin lasted only four seasons in the NBA. And for the last two, he came off the bench behind the top pick in the '74 draft: Walton.

9 Hasheem Thabeet
(2nd overall pick, 2009, Memphis Grizzlies)
You can't teach size, and that's a big reason why the 7' 3" Thabeet was the second pick of the '09 draft. After spending most of his life playing soccer in the African nation of Tanzania, Thabeet developed rapidly while playing college basketball at the University of Connecticut. But his development stopped once he got to the NBA. Thabeet has often been overpowered in the paint, and has shown little on the offensive end of the court. Over his first five NBA seasons, he averaged just over two points per game for the Grizzlies, Houston Rockets, Portland Trail Blazers and Oklahoma City Thunder.

10 Pervis Ellison
(1st overall pick, 1989, Sacramento Kings)
Ellison led the University of Louisville to a national title as a freshman, but he didn't have the same immediate success in the NBA. The Kings gave up on Ellison after an injury-filled rookie year, trading him to Washington after he lasted just 34 games for Sacramento. Ellison actually started to emerge as a force for the Bullets, averaging 20.0 points and 11.2 rebounds in his third season and winning Most Improved Player honors. But a series of injuries took their toll, and Ellison finished his career with just 245 starts and a scoring average of only 9.5 points per game.

TOP 10
CLUTCH

PLAYERS

1 Michael Jordan
Jordan hit 24 game-winning shots for the Chicago Bulls, seven of them coming in postseason games. His most memorable game-winner was from Game 6 of the 1998 NBA Finals. Jordan hit a 20-foot jumper over Byron Russell of the Utah Jazz with 5.2 seconds left to give the Bulls a one-point lead and clinch his sixth and final NBA title.

2 Jerry West
Nicknamed "Mr. Clutch," West's most famous buzzer-beater came on a 60-foot heave in Game 3 of the 1970 Finals that forced overtime. Though he won only one title, he was always at his best in the biggest games. West won the first Finals MVP award ever given out, in 1969, even though the Los Angeles Lakers lost to the Boston Celtics in seven games.

3 Larry Bird
Some of Bird's many Boston Celtics game-winners came with a high degree of difficulty. Like in January 1985 when, with the Celtics trailing the Portland Blazers by a point, Bird made a shot over a defender while falling out of bounds on the baseline. Or in Game 7 of the 1981 Eastern Conference Finals, when his left-handed bank shot clinched the game.

4 Kobe Bryant
Even when he was a teenage rookie, Bryant wanted the last shot, but things didn't go well early when he took them. His rookie year ended with three air balls in the final minutes of a loss to the Utah Jazz. But his skills and confidence grew in the coming years, and he became a clutch shot-maker, especially during the Lakers' last five NBA title runs.

5 Robert Horry
Horry's seven NBA titles, won with three different teams, are more than anyone who didn't play on the Bill Russell Celtics of the 1950s and '60s. While Horry was a role player, he earned the nickname "Big Shot Bob" by making key, last-minute shots in the Finals for the Houston Rockets, Los Angeles Lakers, and San Antonio Spurs.

6 Reggie Miller

Miller's one-man comeback in New York's Madison Square Garden in 1995 stands out. The Indiana Pacers trailed the rival Knicks by six with 18.7 seconds left in Game 1 of the Eastern Conference Finals. Miller hit a three, stole the inbounds pass, ran back behind the arc and hit another three to tie it. The Knicks missed two free throws and a put-back. Miller rebounded, was fouled, and calmly made both shots. The Pacers left the Garden with a two-point win.

7 Paul Pierce

Pierce has always been great at knocking down shots with a hand in his face. It makes him a natural for shooting big shots in big games. He was MVP of the 2008 Finals, leading the rebuilt Boston Celtics past the Los Angeles Lakers. In following years, he hit last-second game-winners in the playoffs against tough defenses like the Chicago Bulls and Miami Heat.

8 Magic Johnson

Magic was the engine that made the "Showtime" Lakers go, leading L.A. to five titles in the 1980s. He made one of the most memorable plays in postseason history against the Boston Celtics in Game 4 of the 1987 Finals. With the Lakers trailing by one, Magic drove against Celtics forward Kevin McHale. His running hook shot with two seconds left won it for L.A.

9 John Havlicek

Havlicek was legendary for his stamina, with non-stop energy giving him an edge late in games. In Game 7 of the 1965 Eastern Conference Finals, his defense sealed the series for the Boston Celtics. He tipped a pass away to prevent a potential game-winner for the Philadelphia 76ers. Nine years later, he tied a record with nine points in one overtime in Game 6 of the '74 Finals.

10 Chauncey Billups

Billups once said the shots he takes at the end of games are just like the ones he takes in the first quarter. His late-game heroics earned him the nickname "Mr. Big Shot." He hit better than 50 percent from the field when the Detroit Pistons upset the Lakers in the 2004 Finals, scoring 21.0 points per game and earning Finals MVP honors.

TOP 10

FUTURE

1 Anthony Davis
Due to his quickness and 7' 4" wingspan, the 6' 10" forward is already an elite shot-blocker for the New Orleans Pelicans. A point guard in high school until he hit a late growth spurt, Davis also has the potential to become a pick-and-roll stopper in the Kevin Garnett mold, making him an elite defensive player. He can score, too. In 2013–14, his second year in the NBA, Davis averaged 20.8 points per game.

2 Kyrie Irving
Irving has been stuck on a rebuilding Cleveland Cavaliers team that hasn't surrounded him with much talent, but there's no denying he's going to be one of the NBA's top point guards over the next decade. Irving has averaged 20.7 points per game through his first three NBA seasons despite coming into the NBA as a 19-year-old. He's also shown the potential to be an elite playmaker with the right supporting cast.

3 Andrew Wiggins
Wiggins is a Toronto native and the son of former NBA player Mitchell Wiggins. Andrew didn't quite live up to the hype in his one season at the University of Kansas in 2013–14, but he was the Big 12 Freshman of the Year and a second-team All-American. He has the skill set to be a star, showing the athleticism that many great players have. If he matches his physical skills with competitive drive, he'll be a star.

4 Bradley Beal
He suffered through an injury-plagued rookie season in 2012–13, but Beal showed in his second season that he is going to be a top NBA shooting guard. Teaming up with point guard John Wall, Beal knocked down more than 40 percent of his threes in his second season, upping his scoring average to 17.1. He's a big reason the Washington Wizards figure to be a perennial playoff team in coming years.

5 Joel Embiid
Embiid grew up playing volleyball in Cameroon, but he has taken to the hardwood in a hurry. Though it was only his third season of organized basketball, the 7-footer emerged as a star at the University of Kansas in 2013–14. His volleyball background explains why he's a great shot-blocker. He has the size, soft shooting touch, and nimble feet to become an All-Star if he keeps improving at this pace.

STARS

6 Jabari Parker
When Parker first appeared on the cover of *Sports Illustrated*, he was playing for Simeon High School in Chicago, and he was called the best high school player since LeBron James. He followed it up with a great freshman season at Duke University in 2013–14, and was named first-team All-America. While Parker needs to improve defensively, he has shown the offensive game to be an NBA star.

7 Andre Drummond
At 6' 10" with a rare combination of strength and athleticism, Drummond has loads of potential. In 2013–14, his second NBA season, he was second in the NBA in rebounding (13.2 per game) and 10th in blocked shots (1.6). He may never be much of an offensive player due to his poor free throw shooting. But if he gets better as a team defender, the Detroit Pistons might have a future NBA Defensive Player of the Year.

8 Jahlil Okafor
Set to play for Duke University in 2014–15, Okafor was the nation's top high school recruit before committing. He's a true center, standing 6' 10", 280 pounds, and Okafor has the nimble feet and soft touch that are rare for a player his size. He dominated in high school All-Star games, earning co-MVP honors at the McDonald's All-American game and Jordan Brand Classic, offering a taste of what he might do at Duke.

9 Jonas Valanciunas
Playing for his native Lithuania as a 19-year-old in 2011, Valanciunas was dominant at times during EuroBasket play. The Raptors saw enough potential to take him fifth overall in the 2011 draft, even though he wouldn't come to the NBA until a full season later. He still has to learn some of the little things, but his power game around the basket could lead to Valanciunas soon becoming an All-Star.

10 Giannis Antetokounmpo
Antetokounmpo came into the 2013 NBA draft as an 18-year-old mystery man. He hadn't played much in higher levels in his native Greece, and NBA teams weren't sure what to think about his raw game. The Milwaukee Bucks took a chance and drafted him 15th overall. While his game remains very raw, the 6' 9" "Greek Freak" also shows the kind of special athleticism that can't be taught.

TOP 10

SCORERS

1 Kareem Abdul-Jabbar

Abdul-Jabbar is the NBA's all-time leading scorer at 38,387 points. At 7' 2", he was simply too big to handle in the paint. Throw in his tremendous athleticism and soft touch on his unblockable skyhook, and you have the most unguardable player in league history.

Karl Malone

Malone was a burly 6'9" power forward, but he was also nimble on his feet. He and Hall of Fame point guard John Stockton perfected the pick-and-roll, accounting for a healthy chunk of The Mailman's 36,928 points, which ranks second on the NBA's all-time scoring list.

Michael Jordan

When Jordan entered the NBA in 1984–85, his biggest strength was his electrifying athleticism. As the years went on, it became clear his greatness came from his work ethic, competitiveness, and ability to adjust as teams defended him differently. His fadeaway jumper was one of the greatest weapons in league history. His Airness owns the all-time records for career scoring average (30.1) and single-season scoring titles (10).

Kobe Bryant

When Kobe was in his prime, he had such a dizzying array of moves that he couldn't be guarded inside the three-point arc. He won back-to-back scoring titles, in 2005–06 and '06–07. His 81 points against the Toronto Raptors on January 22, 2006, is the second-highest single-game total in NBA history.

Wilt Chamberlain

Despite constant double- and triple-teams, the 7'1", 275-pound Chamberlain scored at will. He had the three highest single-season scoring averages in NBA history (50.4 in 1961–62, 44.8 in '62–63, and 38.4 in '60–61). His single-game scoring record of 100 points is unbreakable.

Kevin Durant

Durant is just getting started. In 2009–10, he became the youngest scoring champion in history (21 years, 197 days). And in '13–14, he won his fourth scoring title. At 6'10" with a skill set of an elite shooting guard, he could end up finishing his career as the greatest scorer ever.

Elgin Baylor

Undersized for a forward, the 6'5" Minneapolis/Los Angeles Laker made up for it with athleticism, smarts, and an exceptional shooting touch. Through 2013–14, Baylor owned the fifth-highest career scoring average of all time (27.4) and the fourth-highest single-season average (38.3 in '61–62).

George Gervin

The master of the finger roll, Gervin dominated the ABA, first with the Virginia Squires then with the San Antonio Spurs. The Spurs jumped to the NBA in 1976–77 and the points kept coming for The Iceman. He won four NBA scoring titles over the next six seasons.

Bob McAdoo

If not for injuries, McAdoo might have gone down as the greatest offensive forward of all time. Starring for the Buffalo Braves early in his career, McAdoo won scoring titles in his second, third, and fourth NBA seasons (1973–74 through '75–76). He's one of only seven players to win three straight scoring titles.

Allen Iverson

Standing just 6'0" and weighing only 165 pounds, it's a wonder that Iverson could excel in the NBA. But thanks to his quickness, creativity, and unmatched toughness attacking players a foot taller, The Answer became one of the most prolific scorers in league history. He was a four-time scoring champion and averaged 30 or more points per game in five different seasons.

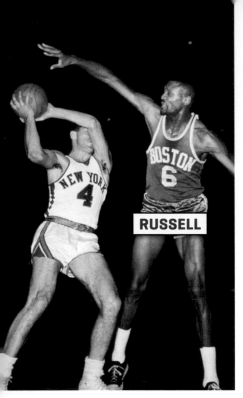

RUSSELL

HOWARD

GARNETT

TOP 10
DEFENDERS

COOPER

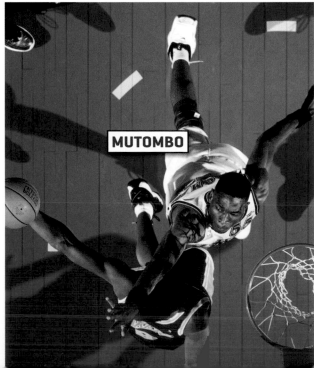

MUTOMBO

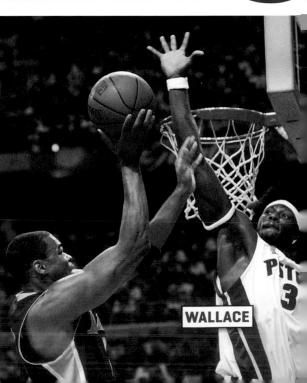

WALLACE

EATON

MONCRIEF

PAYTON

OLAJUWON

1 Bill Russell

Coming into the NBA in 1956, Russell wasn't considered a great offensive player. But the Boston Celtics saw his defense as the missing piece on their team. Along with being a top rebounder, Russell was a phenomenal shot-blocker. Unlike many shot-blockers today, who spike shots out-of-bounds to lose possession, Russell consistently deflected blocks to himself or a teammate. The Celtics had never won a title before Russell entered the league, but they'd go on to win 11 titles in a 13-year span with their defensive star leading the way.

2 Dwight Howard

During the mid-2000s, the Orlando Magic built their entire roster around Howard's defensive capabilities. Orlando loaded up on scorers and shooters who couldn't play a lick of D, knowing that Howard's combination of size, strength and athleticism could make up for their mistakes. It's why he was the only player ever to win the NBA's Defensive Player of the Year award, introduced in 1982–83, three years in a row (2008–09 to '10–11).

3 Kevin Garnett

When he first broke into the NBA as a teenager in 1995–96, Garnett was a great defender because of his length and athleticism. He was 6' 11" but moved as well as some guards. As he picked up on some of the nuances of defense, he became arguably the best ever at stopping basketball's unstoppable play: the pick-and-roll. Garnett's defense was key in leading the Boston Celtics to a title in 2007–08. And even as he slowed down later in his career, he used different tactics to stop opposing pick-and-rollers.

4 Ben Wallace

Undrafted out of Division II Virginia Union University, Wallace seemed unlikely to do much in the NBA because of his limited offensive game. But the 6' 9" power forward brought strength, athleticism, and a ton of energy to the defensive end of the floor. He broke out as a defense-first superstar for the Detroit Pistons in the mid-2000s. Wallace is one of only two players to win the NBA's Defensive Player of the Year award four times.

5 Michael Cooper

The "Showtime" L.A. Lakers of the 1980s had plenty of offensive firepower, but they wouldn't have won five titles without Cooper's defense. His battles with Boston Celtics legend Larry Bird were epic, with Cooper using his 6' 5" frame and quickness to shadow Bird's every step. He was one of the few players who could match Bird's competiveness. Cooper won only one Defensive Player of the Year award, in 1986–87, but should have won more.

6 Dikembe Mutombo

Mutombo is most famous for his blocked shot celebrations. After rejecting an opponent, he would wag his index finger and shake his head "no." It's a move that plenty of players imitate, but Mutombo was the original. And he had plenty of chances to wag that finger. Mutombo's 3,289 career blocks were second all time (the NBA didn't start tracking blocks until 1973–74), and he led the NBA in blocks three straight seasons ('93–94 to '95–96). He also is one of two players to win four Defensive Player of the Year awards, and he did it with three different teams (Denver Nuggets, Atlanta Hawks, and Philadelphia 76ers).

7 Mark Eaton

After not getting much playing time at UCLA, Eaton was a surprise fourth-round pick of the Utah Jazz in 1982. He developed into one of the NBA's greatest shot blockers. He led the league in blocks four times, and he holds blocked shot records for career average (3.5), and single-season average (5.6 in '84–85).

8 Gary Payton

Guarding point guards and shooting guards, Payton's nickname "The Glove" was inspired by the lockdown defense he played on fellow All-Star Kevin Johnson during the 1993 Western Conference Finals. He won the Defensive Player of the Year award in 1995–96, the only point guard to ever win that honor.

9 Sidney Moncrief

Moncrief was ahead of his time in terms of game-planning for opponents. He'd get into his low crouch and force opponents to play to their weaknesses, taking away a favorite move, or a favored hand. The NBA introduced the Defensive Player of the Year award in 1982–83, and Moncrief won it the first two years it was handed out.

10 Hakeem Olajuwon

Olajuwon will always be remembered for his graceful offensive play in the low post. But The Dream put his size, strength, and athleticism to good use on defense too. Olajuwon's 3,830 career rejections are the most in the NBA since the league started tracking blocks in 1973–74. He won back-to-back Defensive Player of the Year awards in '92–93 and '93–94, and anchored the D for a Rockets team that won back-to-back titles in '93–94 and '94–95.

Top 10

DUNKER

63

S

1 Vince Carter

2000 NBA Slam Dunk Contest winner

At All-Star Weekend in 2000, Carter put on the most unforgettable show in Dunk Contest history. "Vinsanity" was in full effect as he threw down two reverse 360 windmills, a "honey dip" (a one-handed dunk, after which he hung from the rim by his elbow), and a between-the-legs dunk off of a bounce pass from his cousin, and Toronto Raptors teammate, Tracy McGrady. No one has ever done it better.

HOWARD

65

ERVING

Gatorade
Gatorade
Slam-Dunk Championship

2 Dominique Wilkins
Two-time NBA Slam Dunk Contest winner (1985 and '90)

Wilkins was one of the most unique dunkers in history. While others opted for creativity and grace, the Atlanta Hawks star went with pure power. Known as "The Human Highlight Film," Wilkins's signature dunk was a windmill thrown down with unmatched quickness and ferocity.

3 Michael Jordan
Two-time NBA Slam Dunk Contest winner (1987 and '88)

Iconic dunks are how the Chicago Bulls legend earned nicknames like "Air Jordan" and "His Airness." Jordan dazzled fans with two wins in the Slam Dunk Contest. The most memorable moment in the contest's history came in 1988. Defending his title against Dominique Wilkins on his home court, Jordan famously clinched the win by taking off from the foul line for a one-handed slam.

4 Julius "Dr. J" Erving
1976 ABA Slam Dunk Contest winner

Dr. J used an unmatched mixture of style and grace to win the 1976 ABA Slam Dunk Contest. His "Rock the Baby" dunk in 1983 remains one of basketball's most iconic in-game slams. As he approached the hoop, Erving clutched the ball against his wrist and swung his arm forward then back before unleashing a monstrous one-handed dunk over Lakers defender Michael Cooper.

5 Dwight Howard
2008 NBA Slam Dunk Contest winner

Howard hasn't always gotten credit for being a great dunker because his height gives him such an advantage, but few can fly like he can. He famously donned a Superman jersey and cape for the clinching dunk at the 2008 Slam Dunk Contest. One year later, he brought out the cape and pulled off one of the most amazing dunks in the competition's history: He threw it down on a special rim that was *12 feet* off the ground!

67

MINER

GRIFFIN

6 **Harold Miner**
Two-time NBA Slam Dunk Contest winner (1993 and '95)
Nicknamed "Baby Jordan," Miner won the 1993 NBA Slam Dunk Contest and described it as the highlight of his rookie season with the Miami Heat. Two years later, Miner joined Michael Jordan and Dominique Wilkins as the third two-time champion of the NBA Slam Dunk Contest.

7 **Blake Griffin**
2011 NBA Slam Dunk Contest winner
Griffin's huge vertical leap and pure power have made him the top dunker in today's NBA. On his home court in Los Angeles in 2011, he clinched the Slam Dunk Contest by leaping over the hood of a car, catching an alley-oop pass from Clippers teammate Baron Davis (who was peeking out through the sun roof), and throwing it down.

8 **Spud Webb**
1986 NBA Slam Dunk Contest winner
In the 1986 NBA Slam Dunk Contest, Webb shocked the world with remarkable athleticism. He lobbed a high bounce pass to himself and finished with a reverse dunk to defeat defending champion and Atlanta Hawks teammate Dominique Wilkins in the event's final. At just 5' 7", Webb remains the shortest player to ever win the dunk contest.

9 **Nate Robinson**
Three-time NBA Slam Dunk Contest winner (2006 and '09, '10)
Going head-to-head against defending champ Dwight Howard in 2009, the 5 '9" Robinson got an assist from his rival. The 6' 11" Howard stood in front of the hoop wearing his Superman cape. Robinson came out in a green Knicks uniform with a bright green ball and dunked over him. Robinson was dubbed "KryptoNate," a play on Superman's one weakness: kryptonite.

10 **Jason Richardson**
Two-time NBA Slam Dunk Contest winner (2002 and '03)
Richardson was a two-footed leaper who powered his way to back-to-back Slam Dunk Contest titles in 2002 and '03. He won in '03 by putting a new spin on the through-the-legs dunk many had pulled off. Richardson started on the baseline, tossed it to himself, passed it from back to front through his legs, and finished with a one-handed reverse jam.

BIG

1 **Wilt Chamberlain: 7' 1"**
Known as "Wilt the Stilt," Chamberlain's size and athleticism allowed him to dominate offensively like no other big man ever has. He ranks second in career scoring average and first in rebounds per game. He even led the NBA in assists one season, when he had 702 in 1967–68. His 100-point game against the New York Knicks on March 2, 1962 stands as basketball's most unbreakable record.

2 **Kareem Abdul-Jabbar: 7' 2"**
Known as Lew Alcindor at UCLA, he was so dominant that the NCAA briefly outlawed dunking. He changed his name to Kareem Abdul-Jabbar after winning the NBA title with the Milwaukee Bucks in his second season, but the game, especially his patented sky hook, remained the same. He's the NBA's all-time leading scorer (38,387 career points), and the league's only six-time MVP.

3 **Shaquille O'Neal: 7' 1"**
Shaq was not only tall, but he was 325 pounds of muscle (at least early in his career) and very athletic. The league has never seen a physical specimen like him. Shaq powered his way through opponents on both ends of the floor. He won four NBA titles, an MVP award (in 1999–2000), and two scoring titles. He also became one of basketball's most beloved personalities off the floor.

4 **Dirk Nowitzki: 7' 0"**
Hall of Fame coach Don Nelson, who drafted Nowitzki, once said that he had never seen a 7-footer who could do the things Nowitzki was able to do. The German forward is a big man with the basketball savvy of a point guard. He's one of the greatest shooters of all time, and his size makes his one-legged fadeaway unstoppable. He's been an MVP in the regular season and the Finals for the Dallas Mavericks.

5 **David Robinson: 7' 1"**
Robinson was known as "The Admiral" because of his time in the United States Navy and his leadership on the court. The San Antonio Spurs drafted him first overall in 1987, but they had to wait two seasons to sign him due to Robinson's service duty. He became a dominant big man on both ends of the floor, a 10-time All-Star who won MVP in 1994–95 and teamed up with Tim Duncan to win two NBA titles.

GUYS

6 Patrick Ewing: 7' 0"
The heart and soul of the New York Knicks in the 1980s and '90s, Ewing was a rock. He was Rookie of the Year in 1985–86, made 11 All-Star teams, and finished in the league's top 10 in scoring eight times. The only thing missing from the Hall of Famer's résumé is a championship. He brought the Knicks oh-so-close in the 1994 Finals before they fell in heartbreaking fashion to the Houston Rockets in seven games.

7 Robert Parish: 7' 0"
Known as "The Chief," Parish was a rising star for the Golden State Warriors before a trade to the Boston Celtics. That's when his career really took off. Teaming up with forwards Larry Bird and Kevin McHale in the greatest frontcourt of all time, Parish helped Boston to three NBA titles. A nine-time All-Star and Hall of Famer, Parish ranks eighth in total rebounds on the NBA's all-time list.

8 Artis Gilmore: 7' 2"
Gilmore dominated the ABA as a member of the Kentucky Colonels, leading that league in rebounding four times in his six seasons. He was the ABA MVP and won Playoff MVP honors when he led Kentucky to the 1974–75 title. He had similar success after jumping to the NBA, a six-time All-Star who held down the low post for both the Chicago Bulls and the San Antonio Spurs.

9 Yao Ming: 7' 6"
The NBA has had players this size, but none of them had the skills and athleticism that Yao had. The Chinese big man became the NBA's first star from the Far East, and he was selected to start in eight NBA All-Star Games for the Houston Rockets. He started to emerge as the league's best true center in the mid-2000s, but then chronic foot injuries eventually cut his career short after just seven full seasons.

10 Dikembe Mutombo: 7' 2"
Mutombo was a game-changer on the defensive end, protecting the rim as well as anyone in league history. He won four Defensive Player of the Year awards, leading the NBA in rebounding twice and total blocked shots per game three times. The eight-time All-Star also became well-known for his humanitarian work in Africa, especially his native Congo.

TOP 10

LITTLE

1 Allen Iverson
Iverson was listed at 6-feet but it never looked that way, especially as he relentlessly challenged big men on the offensive end. He made up for his lack of size with quickness and unmatched toughness. He led the Philadelphia 76ers to the 2001 NBA Finals, consistently lighting up defenses for a team that lacked a legitimate second scoring option. During his 17-year career, Iverson won four scoring titles, and his career 26.7 scoring average ranks seventh all time.

2 Isiah Thomas
The Detroit Pistons of the late 1980s were known as the "Bad Boys" because of their toughness. Their leader, the 6' 1" Thomas, was as tough as any of them. In Game 6 of the 1988 Finals, with a chance to clinch the title against the Los Angeles Lakers, Thomas scored 25 points in the third quarter while playing on a sprained ankle. Detroit lost the game on a controversial late foul call, then lost Game 7. But behind "Zeke," the Pistons broke through for titles in both 1989 and '90.

3 Steve Nash
Nash is a small guard (listed at 6' 3") from a small college (Santa Clara). After two seasons with the Phoenix Suns and then six with the Dallas Mavericks, Nash re-signed with the Suns. When he wasn't weaving through defenses to find open teammates, he was one of the most accurate shooters in NBA history. Nash led a 33-win improvement in his first year back in Phoenix, 2004–05. He won back-to-back MVPs in '04–05 and '05–06.

4 Chris Paul
Standing only 6-feet tall, CP3 is today's premier point guard. He's quick and creative, with one of the best basketball IQs in the league. Through the 2013–14 season, he had made the All-Star team seven consecutive seasons and had led the Clippers to a win percentage of .600 or better in each of his three years with the team. He has led the NBA in assists three times and steals six times. Paul is the only player to lead the league in both those categories two seasons in a row ('07–08 and '08–09).

5 Calvin Murphy
At just 5' 9", Murphy is the shortest player in the Basketball Hall of Fame. At his size, he seemed like a better fit in his first sport: baton twirling (he was a national champion). He ended up starring on the hardwood, first at Niagara University and then for the San Diego / Houston Rockets. Murphy never backed down on the defensive side of the court. He also made 78 consecutive free throw attempts during the 1980–81 season, a record that stood for more than 12 years.

GUYS

6 Mark Price
Price was one of the sweetest shooters in NBA history — he won the Three-Point Shootout twice and made more than 40 percent of his career three-point attempts. A 6-foot point guard with excellent court vision, he spent the first nine of his 12 NBA seasons with the Cleveland Cavaliers. Price was a four-time All-Star and a member of the 1994 U.S. national team, known as Dream Team II, that won the gold medal at the 1994 FIBA World Championship.

7 Ty Lawson
Lawson was the best collegiate point guard in the nation during his last season at the University of North Carolina, leading the Tar Heels to a national title. But his 5' 11" stature caused him to tumble to the 18th overall pick in the 2009 draft. He ended up being a steal for the Denver Nuggets, leading one of the NBA's most explosive offenses. Lawson ranked in the league's top 10 in assists in two of his first three seasons as a full-time starter.

8 Spud Webb
Webb has always been best-known for his victory in the 1986 Slam Dunk Contest. And for good reason: At 5' 7", it's amazing Webb could dunk at all, let alone elevate high enough to throw down the acrobatic slams needed to win the event. He was more than just a dunker though. Webb averaged double-digit points for five straight seasons over the first half of the 1990s, and he twice averaged seven-plus assists for the Sacramento Kings.

9 Tyrone "Muggsy" Bogues
The NBA has never seen a player like Muggsy Bogues, who at 5' 3" is the smallest man ever to step onto an NBA court. Bogues's small stature actually helped make him great. Because he was so low to the ground, he could consistently get into the paint and create scoring chances for teammates. He finished in the league's top five in assists in five different seasons, and ranks among the NBA's all-time top 20 in both total assists (6,726) and assists per game (7.6).

10 Nate Robinson
A two-sport star at the University of Washington (he was a starting cornerback on the football team as a freshman), Robinson's athleticism and toughness have translated onto the hardcourt. During the 2013 playoffs, he averaged 16.3 points per game for an injury-plagued Chicago Bulls team that made it to the Eastern Conference semifinals. And despite his 5' 9" frame, he's a dazzling dunker. In 2010, he became the NBA's first three-time Slam Dunk champion.

TOP 10 HIGH SCHOOL TO NBA

1 LeBron James

When he was 17 years old, James appeared on the cover of *Sports Illustrated*, which dubbed him "The Chosen One." It seemed crazy to put those expectations on a high schooler, but the star from St. Vincent-St. Mary in Akron, Ohio, has certainly lived up to the hype. The Cleveland Cavaliers made him the first pick of the 2003 draft, and James went on to pile up four NBA Most Valuable Player awards before the age of 30. He is a gifted all-around talent who could very well end his career as the greatest player in league history.

2 Kobe Bryant

During a pre-draft workout for the Los Angeles Lakers, a 17-year-old Bryant dominated against retired Lakers Larry Drew and Michael Cooper. General manager Jerry West knew that the kid from Lower Merion High School in Pennsylvania was his man. The Lakers made a pre-draft deal with the Charlotte Hornets, who selected Bryant with the 13th pick and traded him to L.A. for center Vlade Divac. After a rocky rookie season, Kobe developed into one of the most complete offensive players the NBA has ever seen.

3 Kevin Garnett

When Garnett declared for the 1995 NBA draft out of Farragut Academy in Chicago, he was the first high school player in two decades to make the jump directly to the pros. The Minnesota Timberwolves selected him fifth overall, and the teen became a starter halfway through his rookie year. He developed into a dominant defensive player with a versatile offensive game. He's a 15-time All-Star, was the league's MVP in 2003–04, and led the Boston Celtics to a championship in '07–08, his first year with the team.

4 Dwight Howard

Coming out of Southwest Atlanta Christian Academy in 2004, Howard was long, skinny, and athletic. Many thought he was the next Kevin Garnett. After being drafted first overall by the Orlando Magic, Howard bulked up big-time. He became a more dominating defensive presence than Garnett, even if he could never match KG's offensive skills. The defense, shot-blocking, and rebounding earned him three straight Defensive Player of the Year awards, from 2008–09 to '10–11.

5 Moses Malone

The 6' 10" Malone was a man among boys at Petersburg (Virginia) High School. So when he was drafted by the Utah Stars of the American Basketball Association in 1974, he decided to turn pro. "He's so quick, it's unbelievable," said Bucky Buckwalter, the Stars' coach who was responsible for luring Malone away from a commitment to the University of Maryland. Malone ended up in the NBA when the league merged with the ABA in 1976. He made a combined 14 All-Star appearances during a Hall of Fame career.

6 Tracy McGrady

The Toronto Raptors took McGrady, a high schooler at Mount Zion Christian Academy in North Carolina, with the ninth pick of the 1997 draft. But T-Mac's career didn't really take off until he signed with the Orlando Magic three years later. He averaged 25-plus points per game in each of his four seasons with Orlando, winning back-to-back scoring titles in 2002–03 and '03–04. He went on to star for the Houston Rockets, but a series of injuries cut his prime years short.

7 Jermaine O'Neal

O'Neal seemed overwhelmed early in his career. After the Portland Trail Blazers drafted him 17th overall out of Eau Claire High School in South Carolina, O'Neal averaged 3.9 points over four seasons with Portland. But the light turned on after a trade to the Indiana Pacers before the 2000–01 season. O'Neal developed into a dominant force in the post on both ends of the floor, winning Most Improved Player honors in '01–02 and making six All-Star appearances.

8 Amar'e Stoudemire

Stoudemire attended five different high schools, ending up at Cypress Creek High in Orlando, where he was Florida's Mr. Basketball in 2002. He made the jump to the pros after that season, and the Phoenix Suns drafted him ninth overall. Though he was raw, Stoudemire still thrived thanks to his athleticism and explosiveness, earning Rookie of the Year honors in 2002–03. He developed into a six-time All-Star before knee problems started to take their toll on him once he reached his early 30s.

9 Darryl Dawkins

After leading Maynard Evans High to a state title in 1974–75, Dawkins declared for the NBA draft as a hardship candidate. The Philadelphia 76ers made him the fifth overall pick, and the 6' 11", 250-pound Dawkins took a few years to find his footing. He averaged double-digit points in nine consecutive seasons, five with the Sixers and four with the New Jersey Nets. But "Chocolate Thunder" is best remembered for his monstrous dunks. He once shattered the backboard twice in a three-week span.

10 Josh Smith

The Atlanta Hawks, Smith's hometown team, selected him 17th overall in the 2004 draft. It was considered a risky choice at the time, but it turned out to be a good one. Smith's rare athleticism has made him one of the most versatile stars in the NBA, attacking the basket with highlight reel dunks on offense and becoming a shot-blocking force on defense. "J-Smoove" signed with the Detroit Pistons after nine years in Atlanta. Through his first 10 seasons, he averaged 15.5 points, 7.9 rebounds, and 2.1 blocks.

SINGLE-GAME
REGULAR-SEASON
PERFORMANCES

1 Wilt Chamberlain, March 2, 1962

The game wasn't televised. No one can find any footage of it. But the 4,000 fans in Hershey, Pennsylvania, will always remember what they saw. New York Knicks center Phil Jordan was out sick, and New York had no answer for Chamberlain. The Philadelphia Warriors star shot 36-for-63 from the field and 28-for-32 from the line, finishing with 100 points. Warriors statistician Harvey Pollack borrowed a piece of paper from a reporter and scribbled "100" on it. Associated Press photographer Paul Vathis, attending the game as a fan, snapped the above photo. It's the one lasting image from the greatest performance in NBA history.

2 Karl Malone, January 27, 1990

It wasn't just that the Utah Jazz star dropped 61 points against the Milwaukee Bucks in this game — after all, other players have scored 60 in a game. It was how easily and efficiently Malone got his buckets. For the most part, he simply lined up on the low block and bullied his way to the basket. But he also got cute in the second half, even stepping out to make a long two (he thought it was a three, but his toe was on the arc). The Mailman shot 21-for-26 from the field and 19-for-23 from the line, and also grabbed 18 rebounds. And since Utah absolutely ran away with the 144–96 victory, he did it all in just 33 minutes of play.

3 Nate Thurmond
October 18, 1974

Only four times in NBA history has a player recorded a quadruple-double — double-digits in four different stat categories. And the first quadruple-double was by Thurmond. An offseason acquisition who was making his Chicago Bulls debut, Thurmond had 22 points, 14 rebounds, 13 assists, and 12 blocks in a 120–115 overtime victory against the Atlanta Hawks. "You have to love defense to get a quadruple double," he said. "There's no way around it."

4 Kobe Bryant
January 22, 2006

It's been accepted that no one will ever top Wilt Chamberlain's NBA-record 100-point game. But on this night against the Toronto Raptors, Kobe came closer than anyone ever has. With the Lakers trailing by as many as 18 points in the second half on their home floor, Bryant started scoring in every way imaginable. He had 27 in the third quarter and 28 in the fourth. When it was over, he had 81 points (28-for-46 from the field, 18-for-20 at the line) in a 122–104 victory.

5 Scott Skiles
December 30, 1990

In their second season in existence, the Orlando Magic were 6–23 and not a very interesting team. But in this game, journeyman point guard Scott Skiles gave Orlando fans a reason to get excited. Skiles, who had taken over as a starter one month into the season, led a near-perfect offensive performance against the Denver Nuggets. The Magic rolled up 155 points with Skiles scoring 22 and, more notably, setting an NBA record with 30 assists in a victory.

6 Michael Jordan
March 28, 1990

Big statistical performances often come in blowouts. But in a late-season battle against the rival Cleveland Cavaliers, the Chicago Bulls needed every one of Jordan's career-high 69 points. MJ's night was efficient, as he shot 23-for-37 from the field and 21-for-23 from the line. Eight of his points came in overtime, equalling the Cavs' OT total, in a 117–113 win. He also got it done on the boards, grabbing a game-high 18 rebounds on the night.

7 David Robinson
April 24, 1994

When Robinson faced the Los Angeles Clippers in the regular-season finale, he had a scoring title in his sights. The San Antonio Spurs fed their star non-stop, and The Admiral didn't waste opportunities. He shot 26-for-41 from the field and 18-for-25 from the line, finishing with 71 points. It's one of only 10 times that an NBA player has scored 70 or more points in a game. Robinson's 29.8 points per game edged Orlando Magic center Shaquille O'Neal (29.3) for the scoring title.

8 Kevin Love
November 12, 2010

It wasn't a promising start for the Minnesota Timberwolves star, who grabbed only two rebounds in the first quarter against the New York Knicks. He didn't even score his first points until four minutes into the second quarter. But Love exploded for 11 points and 15 rebounds in the third quarter alone, rallying the Timberwolves from a 21-point deficit. By the end of the game, he had 31 points and 31 rebounds, the NBA's first 30-30 game in 28 seasons.

9 David Thompson
April 9, 1978

Thompson was chasing George Gervin for the scoring title going into the Denver Nuggets' final game against the Detroit Pistons. He scored 32 points in the first quarter, an NBA record. He had 53 points by halftime. Thompson would end up with 73 points for the game. Unfortunately for him, Gervin re-set the single-quarter scoring record with 33 second-quarter points later that day. He finished with 63, winning the scoring title, 27.22 to 27.15 points per game.

10 Wilt Chamberlain
November 24, 1960

The rivalry between Wilt Chamberlain and Bill Russell was just getting started in 1960–61, Wilt's second NBA season. On this night, Chamberlain beat Russell at his own game. He dominated the paint and pulled down 55 rebounds, an NBA record that still stands. He also added 34 points. Though his Philadelphia Warriors team lost a close one, Chamberlain later said he considered this game more important than his 100-point performance.

—TOP 10—
FAMILIES

1 Rick, Brent, and Jon Barry
A star during the 1960s and '70s, Rick's underhand foul shots were legendary. Four of his sons were pros too. Most notably, Brent won two NBA titles with the San Antonio Spurs and the 1996 Slam Dunk Contest. Jon had a 14-year NBA career and is now a commentator.

2 Cheryl and Reggie Miller
Cheryl is a women's hoops legend. She was a superstar at USC, though knee injuries cut her pro career short. Little brother Reggie was one of the best shooters in NBA history. He was a five-time All-Star during the 1980s and '90s for the Indiana Pacers.

3 Joe and Kobe Bryant
Nicknamed "Jellybean," Joe was a solid power forward during the 1970s and '80s, mostly for the Philadelphia 76ers and San Diego Clippers. He later became a star in Europe. He's now best-known as Kobe's dad. His son is a five-time NBA champion who will go down as one of the game's all-time greats.

4 Dell, Stephen, and Seth Curry
Dell was instant offense during the 1980s and '90s, winning Sixth Man of the Year honors in 1993–94. Steph is a Golden State All-Star who holds the NBA's single-season record for threes. Seth, who was a sharpshooter at Duke, is looking to break into the NBA.

5 Bill and Luke Walton
A versatile big man who may have been even better if not for injury problems, Bill is the only player in league history to have won both MVP and Sixth Man of the Year honors. Son Luke was a versatile forward and key contributor off the bench for two Los Angeles Lakers championship teams.

6 Marc and Pau Gasol
These brothers were traded for each other when the Lakers acquired Pau for a package that included the draft rights to younger brother Marc. Pau is a four-time All-Star who helped the Lakers to two titles. Marc is a star in Memphis, a skilled center and the Defensive Player of the Year in 2012–13.

7 Dominique and Gerald Wilkins
Dominique was a prolific scorer. The Hall of Famer was a nine-time All-Star during the 1980s and '90s, and won two Slam Dunk Contests. Little brother Gerald was a top defensive stopper. The two played their final season together, with the Orlando Magic in 1998–99.

8 Stan and Kevin Love
The Baltimore Bullets selected Stan ninth overall in the 1971 draft, but the power forward lasted only five pro seasons as a hard-working reserve. His son has made a bigger mark. One of the NBA's top rebounders, Kevin has made multiple All-Star teams and won the Three-Point Shootout in 2012.

9 Tom and Dick Van Ardsdale
These identical twins had nearly identical success in the NBA during the 1960s and '70s. The swingmen were both three-time All-Stars, Dick with the Phoenix Suns and Tom with the Cincinnati Royals. Tom joined Dick in Phoenix in 1976–77, their final season.

10 Bernard and Albert King
Bernard was an unstoppable scorer for five different teams, including the New York Knicks and Golden State Warriors. The Hall of Famer won a scoring title in 1984–85. Younger brother Albert had a solid nine-season run in the NBA, mostly with the New Jersey Nets.

TOP 10

SIXTH MEN

1 Manu Ginobili

Ginobili has started 70 or more games in a season twice in his career (2004–05 and '10–11), and he was an All-Star in both of those seasons. But San Antonio Spurs coach Gregg Popovich found Ginobili's high-energy, aggressive play was most effective off the bench. It allows Ginobili to take advantage of weary starters and less-talented bench players, and also keeps him fresh for the postseason. After playing a smaller role in San Antonio's 2003 title run, Ginobili was a key cog coming off the bench for two of the Spurs' championship runs (2005, '07). He won Sixth Man of the Year honors in '07–08.

2 Kevin McHale

A Hall of Famer and one of the best power forwards in league history, McHale was a three-time NBA champion and a seven-time All-Star for the Boston Celtics. But before he joined Larry Bird and Robert Parish to form one of the greatest starting frontcourts of all time, McHale came off the bench as Boston's sixth man. He was a scoring and rebounding machine, averaging 18.4 points and 7.4 rebounds in 1983–84, then 19.8 and 9.0 in '84–85. He won Sixth Man of the Year honors both seasons.

3 James Harden

Before Harden became a franchise player for the Houston Rockets, he came off the bench for the Oklahoma City Thunder. The third member of the Thunder's Big Three, along with Kevin Durant and Russell Westbrook, Harden was a prolific scorer. But he was also a solid ball-handler and savvy playmaker, taking some of the heat off Westbrook, a shoot-first point guard. In 2011–12, Harden averaged 16.8 points per game for OKC, winning Sixth Man of the Year honors.

4 Detlef Schrempf

Schrempf did it all for the Indiana Pacers in the early '90s. He was a 6' 10" forward who could score and rebound, but could also run the offense as a passer and playmaker. Between 1990–91 and '91–92, he averaged 16.7 points, 8.8 rebounds, 3.8 assists, and became the second player (along with Kevin McHale) to win Sixth Man of the Year honors in back-to-back seasons. Schrempf moved into the starting lineup after that and went on to play in three All-Star games.

5 Ricky Pierce

Pierce was one of the best sixth man scorers in league history. In 1986–87, he averaged 19.5 points per game as the Milwaukee Bucks' top reserve. In '89–90, he finished 16th in the NBA with a scoring average of 23.0 points per game despite playing an average of only 29.0 minutes per game. Pierce won Sixth Man of the Year honors in both of those seasons, and in 1991 he made the All-Star team despite the fact that he was still coming off the bench in Milwaukee.

6 Jamal Crawford

Crawford is a dazzling ball-handler who scores points in bunches when he gets on a hot streak. After starting games for most of the first half of his career, he signed with the Atlanta Hawks before the 2009–10 season and was tried as a sixth man. Crawford thrived in the role, earning Sixth Man of the Year honors after averaging 18.0 points per game. He won his second Sixth Man of the Year award after averaging 18.6 points per game for the Los Angeles Clippers in '13–14.

7 Jason Terry

A starting point guard for the first half of his career, Terry found his niche later as a high-scoring sixth man. The Dallas Mavericks moved JET to the bench during the 2007–08 season. He responded by winning Sixth Man of the Year honors a year later, averaging 19.6 points per game as a reserve. Terry emerged as a key player during the Mavs' championship run in '10–11. In the Finals that year, he scored 27 points in a series-clinching win over the Miami Heat.

8 Clifford Robinson

Robinson was a key reserve on a Portland Blazers team that made the NBA Finals in Robinson's first (1989–90) and third ('91–92) seasons. A versatile defender in the post, Robinson improved rapidly on the offensive end. In '92–93, he earned Sixth Man of the Year honors after averaging 19.1 points and 6.6 rebounds, helping the Blazers to a fourth consecutive 50-win season. Robinson moved into the starting lineup and made the All-Star team a year later.

9 Eddie Johnson

A lanky scorer who played for six different franchises during a 17-year NBA career, Johnson was a successful starter for the Kansas City / Sacramento Kings and Phoenix Suns before enjoying the best year of his career as a Suns reserve in 1988–89. He shot a career-best 49.7 percent from the field and 41.3 percent on three-pointers that season. Johnson averaged 21.5 points per game and won Sixth Man of the Year honors.

10 John Starks

The hard-nosed Starks had an up-and-down career in New York during the 1990s. He was an all-defensive team selection in 1992–93, and an All-Star the next season. Starks was sent to the bench when the Knicks signed star shooting guard Allan Houston before the '96–97 season, and he responded by averaging 13.8 points, including nearly two three-pointers per game, and playing his typical tough defense. It earned him Sixth Man of the Year honors.

TOP 10
REBOUNDERS

1 Wilt Chamberlain

"Wilt the Stilt" was unmatched on the boards. He was 7' 1", 275 pounds, and athletic. He is the NBA's all time leader in rebounding average (22.9 per game) and total rebounds (23,924). Chamberlain led the NBA in rebounding 11 times. No one else has ever been the top rebounder as many as seven times.

2 Bill Russell

Russell was the one big guy who could go head-to-head with Wilt Chamberlain. Russell and Chamberlain are the only two players in league history to average more than 20 rebounds per game (22.5 for Russell) and total more than 20,000 rebounds (21,620).

3 Dennis Rodman

Rodman made doing the dirty work his job. Standing only 6' 7", Rodman's game was all about energy. He led the NBA in rebounding seven times, more than anyone in league history aside from Wilt Chamberlain.

4 Moses Malone

Malone was known as the "Chairman of the Boards" for good reason. He was impossible to keep off the offensive glass. Since the NBA started tracking offensive rebounds in 1973–74, Malone grabbed more offensive boards per game (5.1) than anyone.

5 Dwight Howard
Howard has a combination of size, strength, and athleticism that is unmatched in NBA history. He is 6' 11" with a vertical leap measured at nearly 40 inches, extremely rare for a big man. It's a big reason why he led the league in rebounding in five of his first 10 NBA seasons.

6 Kevin Love
Love is wide-bodied, strong, and simply has a knack for reading where shots are coming off of the rim. In 2010–11, his first full season as a starter, he became the first player in eight years to grab an average of more than 15 rebounds per game (15.2).

7 Charles Barkley
Nicknamed the "Round Mound of Rebound," the 250-pound Barkley outmuscled opponents on the boards. He played 16 NBA seasons — eight with the Philadelphia 76ers, four with the Phoenix Suns, and four with the Houston Rockets — and averaged 10 or more rebounds per game all but once.

8 Wes Unseld

Unseld wasn't just one of the greatest ever at clearing the boards, averaging 14.0 rebounds per game during his career (sixth all time). He was also known for turning defensive rebounds into instant offense by snapping long outlet passes to Washington Bullets teammates with pinpoint accuracy.

9 Bob Pettit

Pettit was known more for his scoring prowess, but few forwards in NBA history have worked the boards as hard as he did. Pettit ranks third all time in career rebounds per game (16.2), and Bill Russell once said Pettit is the reason "second effort" became a basketball term.

10 Kevin Garnett

Garnett did just about everything for the Minnesota Timberwolves during the mid-2000's, and that included grabbing tons of boards. He led the NBA in rebounding four seasons in a row (2003–04 to '06–07), one of only four players in NBA history to pull off the feat.

TOP 10
SHOOTERS

1 Stephen Curry

Sharpshooting runs in the Curry family: Stephen's father, Dell, was a high-scoring NBA sixth man who hit more than 40 percent of his threes over 16 seasons. Steph's shooting stroke is flawless. He made 44 percent of his threes over his first five seasons, ranking third all time in three-point percentage. The 272 threes he made in 2012–13 is a single-season record.

2 Ray Allen

No one has hit more career threes than Allen, who knocked down 2,973 over 18 seasons through 2013–14. The Boston Celtics acquired him before the '07–08 season, and he helped lead them to an NBA title. The following season, Allen shot a career-best 95.2 percent from the free throw line.

3 Reggie Miller

Miller's legs flailed and his arms often crossed on his follow-through, but the unique form didn't keep him from being an all-time great shooter. Through the end of 2013–14, Miller and Ray Allen were the only players to hit more than 2,000 career threes (2,560 for Miller).

4 Steve Nash

Nash's elite ball-handling skills were made even more dangerous by his accurate outside shooting. He's had four 50-40-90 seasons (50 percent or better from the field, 40 percent or better on three-pointers, 90 percent or better from the free throw line), more than any other player in NBA history.

5 Larry Bird

Many great shooters benefited from playing alongside superior players. That was never the case with Bird, who was always the Number 1 focus for opposing defenses. His ability to make difficult shots was unmatched. He won the NBA's first three Three-Point Shootouts.

6 Kyle Korver

Korver is as consistent a long-range shooter as there is in today's NBA. He once had a streak of 127 games with at least one three-pointer made; no one else has gotten to even 90 straight games. He also holds the single-season record for three-point percentage, hitting 53.6 percent from behind the arc for the Utah Jazz in 2009–10.

7 Peja Stojakovic

Stojakovic was a sharpshooter from all areas of the floor, especially the corner. He was a three-time All-Star and won the Three-Point Shootout in back-to-back years (2002 and '03). He led the league in three-pointers made with 240 as a member of the Sacramento Kings in 2003–04.

8 Steve Kerr

Kerr stuck around the league for 15 seasons as a bench player because he was so accurate from beyond the three-point arc. He is the NBA's all-time leader in three-point accuracy at 45.4 percent, and his sharpshooting helped his teams win five NBA titles, three with the Chicago Bulls and two with the San Antonio Spurs.

9 Dirk Nowitzki

The NBA has never had a big man who could shoot like Nowitzki. His one-legged fadeaway is one of the most unstoppable shots in NBA history; it's unblockable and he rarely misses. Through 2013–14, Nowitzki had shot 40 percent or better on three-pointers in four different seasons, and 90 percent or better from the line three times.

10 Craig Hodges

Hodges led the NBA in three-point percentage in his fourth season (45.1 percent for the Milwaukee Bucks), and again two years later (49.1 percent for the Bucks and Phoenix Suns). After joining the Chicago Bulls, Hodges won three NBA Three-Point Shootouts (1990–92), joining Larry Bird as the only three-time winner.

1

Michael Jordan in Game 5 of the 1997 NBA Finals

The Utah Jazz had rallied to win Games 3 and 4, tying the NBA Finals, 2–2. The Chicago Bulls got even more bad news the night before Game 5: Living legend Michael Jordan was very sick, suffering from the stomach flu. He arrived at the arena late, looking weak. The Jazz jumped out to a 36–20 lead in the second quarter before Jordan got it going. He scored 17 points in the second to close the gap to four at halftime. With Chicago trailing, 85–84, in the final minute, Jordan went to the line. He made the first shot and missed the second, but the rebound was tipped out to him. He re-set the offense, got the ball back, and knocked down a three-pointer for his 38th point, a shot that proved to be the game-winner. During a time out toward the end of the game, Jordan collapsed into fellow All-Star Scottie Pippen's arms as the two left the court.

SINGLE-GAME POSTSEASON PERFORMANCES

2 Magic Johnson in Game 6 of 1980 NBA Finals

If the Los Angeles Lakers were going to clinch their first NBA title in eight years, they'd have to do it without league MVP Kareem Abdul-Jabbar. The superstar center injured his ankle in Game 5 and wouldn't be able to go as the series headed back to Philadelphia. Head coach Paul Westhead had an idea: Magic Johnson, his 6' 9" rookie point guard, would start the game at center. Johnson played everywhere and did everything that night, finishing with 42 points, 15 rebounds, and seven assists as L.A. beat the 76ers, 123–107. Because of his remarkable effort in Game 6, Johnson is the only rookie to ever win NBA Finals MVP honors.

3 LeBron James in Game 6 of 2012 Eastern Conference Finals

The criticism of LeBron James was getting louder. The NBA's most talented player, James was in his ninth NBA season but had yet to win a title, even after joining fellow stars Dwyane Wade and Chris Bosh one season earlier. Many were, unfairly, saying that James couldn't win big games. That changed after this one. The Heat were facing elimination on the road against the rival Boston Celtics, who had one of the NBA's elite defenses. James shot 19-for-26 from the field and scored 45 points in a dominant 98–79 win, forcing a Game 7 in Miami that the Heat went on to win. Two weeks later, James won the first championship of his career.

4 Reggie Miller in Game 5 of the 1994 Eastern Conference Finals

Miller and the Pacers trailed, 70–58, after three quarters at New York's Madison Square Garden. That's when Miller took over. Constantly jawing with famous filmmaker Spike Lee, a courtside regular at Knicks games, Miller started draining long three after long three. By the time the final horn sounded, he had 25 fourth-quarter points (the Knicks' entire team scored only 16 in the quarter), 39 points for the game, and the Pacers had a 93–86 victory.

5 Bill Russell in Game 7 of the 1962 NBA Finals

The Boston Celtics and Los Angeles Lakers have met in the Finals 11 times, and 1962 was the first time. In Game 7 in Boston, Russell was at his best. He scored four of his team-high 30 points down the stretch in regulation, but L.A. still came back to force overtime. In OT, Russell helped smother Lakers star Elgin Baylor and continued to grab rebounds at an incredible rate (40 for the game, tying his own Finals record). Boston clinched the title with a 110–107 win.

6 Charles Barkley in Game 3 of a 1994 first-round playoff series

Barkley had been suffering back problems throughout the 1993–94 season. With his Phoenix Suns leading the Golden State Warriors, 2–0 in their opening-round best-of-five series, it seemed like a good time to take it easy. Instead, Barkley dominated. In a see-saw battle, he carried the Suns with 56 points on 23-for-31 shooting from the field, plus 14 rebounds. Behind Sir Charles, Phoenix clinched the series sweep with a 140–133 victory.

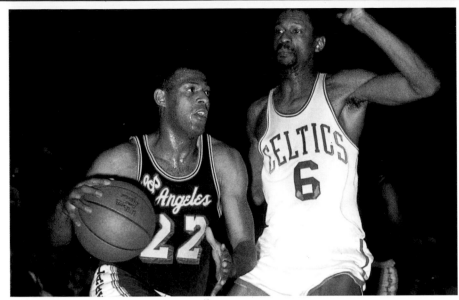

7 Elgin Baylor in Game 5 of the 1962 NBA Finals

Between center Bill Russell and forward Satch Sanders, the Celtics had two of the NBA's elite defenders. They figured they could hold Baylor, the Los Angeles Lakers' star forward, in check by taking turns guarding him one-on-one. (They didn't want to double-team him — Baylor was such a good passer that he could burn them by setting up teammates.) With the series tied 2–2, Baylor was unstoppable in Game 5 in Boston. He scored from spots all over the court, finishing with 61 points, still a Finals record. Sanders summed it up best: "Elgin was just a machine in that game."

8 Michael Jordan in Game 2 of a 1986 first-round playoff series

Jordan played only 18 games during the regular season due to a broken foot. In fact, some in the Bulls' organization thought he shouldn't play in the postseason to make sure his foot was fully healed. MJ put on a show in Game 1, scoring 49 points. That was nothing compared to Game 2. He scored from all over, carrying the Bulls on his back as they pushed the Boston Celtics to double overtime. Boston held on for a 135–131 win, but not before Jordan piled up 63 points, still a playoff record. "I think it's just God disguised as Michael Jordan," Celtics star Larry Bird said afterward.

9 Bob Pettit in Game 6 of the 1958 NBA Finals

After losing to the Boston Celtics in the 1957 NBA Finals, Pettit was a man on a mission for the rematch. With a 3–2 series lead, one last game on their home court, and Celtics star Bill Russell hampered by a sprained ankle, the Hawks needed to strike in Game 6. Pettit had 19 points at halftime and faced a wave of triple teams in the second half. He only got better. With Atlanta clinging to a one-point lead in the final seconds, Pettit tipped in a shot to seal the game. He scored 18 of St. Louis's final 21 points, finishing with 50. It is the only title the Hawks have ever won.

10 LeBron James in Game 5 of the 2007 Eastern Conference Finals

It was a pivotal game for a young LeBron James. He and the Cleveland Cavaliers were on the road against the Detroit Pistons, one of the toughest defensive teams in the NBA, with their series tied 2–2. It was time for The King to prove himself. In a tightly contested game, James carried the Cavs through four quarters and overtime. With the score tied as time winded down in the second OT, James attacked the basket and finished a tough layup with 2.2 seconds left. It was the game-winner and the 48th point for James, who scored Cleveland's final 25 points.

TOP TRIPLE-DOUBLE THREATS 10

1 Oscar Robertson

While big, strong, do-it-all guards have become common in today's NBA, Robertson was a unique and special talent in the 1960s. A huge point guard (6' 5", 205 pounds), he did whatever he wanted on the court. He *averaged* a triple-double in 1961–62 (30.8 points, 12.5 rebounds, 11.4 assists) and finished his career with a record 181 triple-doubles — no one has come within 40 of that record. The Big O's 41 triple-doubles in '61–62 are a single-season record.

2 Magic Johnson

Johnson's do-it-all game fueled the "Showtime" Los Angeles Lakers of the 1980s. At 6' 9" and 220 pounds, he could rebound like a power forward, and played all five positions for L.A. He was an incredibly creative passer, and his height gave him the added advantage of being able to see over defenders. Magic is the NBA's all-time leader in assists per game (11.2), and he ranks second to Oscar Robertson with 138 triple-doubles in his career.

3 Jason Kidd

Kidd was one of the best rebounding guards to ever play. Along with his size (6' 4", 220 pounds), he had a great feel for knowing where a missed shot would carom. He'd grab a board and then transition his team into a fastbreak offense, showing the natural vision and passing skills of an elite point guard. Along with Oscar Robertson and Magic Johnson, Kidd is one of only three players in NBA history with 100 career triple-doubles (107).

4 Wilt Chamberlain

Chamberlain was remembered for scoring (30.1 points per game, second all time) and rebounding (22.9 per game, first all time). But when Alex Hannum became the Philadelphia 76ers' coach in 1966–67, he emphasized passing, and the big man became a playmaker. He averaged 8.2 assists in two seasons playing for Hannum. Wilt's 78 triple-doubles are fourth-most in NBA history.

5 Larry Bird

Larry Legend averaged 24.3 points and 10.0 rebounds for his career. Along with being an elite shooter, he was a smooth ball-handler with an incredible basketball IQ. His 6.3 assists per game are second-most all time for a player 6' 9" or taller. Bird's 59th and final career triple-double, coming in his final NBA season, was a 49-point, 14-rebound, 12-assist game against the Portland Trail Blazers on March 15, 1992.

6 LeBron James

At 6' 8" and 250 pounds, LeBron is built more like an oversized football linebacker than an NBA floor general. But that size, along with his explosive athleticism and elite basketball IQ, is what allowed him to collect 37 triple-doubles during his first 11 pro seasons. And that's only regular season. King James has 11 more in the playoffs, and became the third player in NBA history to have a triple-double in his playoff debut.

7 Lafayette Lever

"Fat" Lever was actually skinny — he was 6' 3" and 170 pounds. But that slight build didn't keep him from becoming one of the best rebounding guards in league history. He led the Denver Nuggets in rebounding three times. He had 43 career triple-doubles, sixth-most all time (through the 2013–14 season). He had 16 triple-doubles in 1986–87; only Oscar Robertson, Wilt Chamberlain, and Magic Johnson had more in a single season.

8 Grant Hill

There's one question that pops up when you look back on Hill's career: What if he stayed healthy? Unfortunately, the star forward was limited because of ankle injuries. At one point during his prime, he played just 47 games over a four-year span. But when healthy, the 6' 8" athletic Hill showed a truly special all-around game. He had 29 career triple-doubles, including a whopping 24 over his first three seasons alone.

9 John Havlicek

A sixth man early in his career, Havlicek had a habit of giving incredible effort every second he was on the floor for the Boston Celtics. A 6' 5" shooting guard, he was a non-stop bundle of energy. Havlicek hit the boards hard, and he might have had a few more triple-doubles if he didn't play alongside rebounding machine Bill Russell. Havlicek also became a floor general for Boston later in his career, and collected 30 triple-doubles.

10 Michael Jordan

Arguably the greatest player of all time, Jordan did everything well. While he was most often leaned upon as the main scorer during the Bulls' run to six NBA championships, Jordan was a triple-double machine earlier in his career. He had a run of seven straight games with a triple-double during the 1988–89 season, tied for the second-longest streak in NBA history. He finished that season with 15, the 10th-most ever in a year.

Top 10
FANS

1 Sacramento Kings

In the early 2000s, when the Kings and Lakers were the best in the West, L.A. coach Phil Jackson called Sacramento a "cow town." So fans brought cowbells to games, filling already-loud Arco Arena with even more noise. The team has struggled for most of the last decade, and nearly relocated multiple times. But as long as the Kings call California's capital home, these fans will remain the loudest and proudest.

2 Chicago Bulls
Six NBA titles might not have been possible without some of the loudest fans in the league. Chicago led the NBA in home attendance from 2009–10 to '13–14.

3 San Antonio Spurs
Spurs fans appreciate their team's consistent success. With their support, San Antonio has won more than 80 percent of its regular-season home games during the Tim Duncan era.

4 Oklahoma City Thunder
Oklahoma City may be a small market, but these fans generate some big-time noise. The "blue-out" helps give Thunder home games a spirited atmosphere.

5 Phoenix Suns
Maybe it's the desert heat, but when Suns fans get into a game, there are few places tougher for an opposing team.

6 Boston Celtics
Boston fans have always had plenty to cheer for. That was especially true in 1985–86, when the Celtics became the only team in history to win 40 home games in one regular season.

7 Golden State Warriors
The atmosphere in Oakland gets crazy, especially when the playoffs roll around.

8 Utah Jazz
The Jazz consistently draw big crowds, even in rebuilding years. Loud fans, plus the thin air of Salt Lake City, make this a tough road trip.

9 Dallas Mavericks
With owner Mark Cuban doubling as a super fan, the fans in Big D make some *big* noise.

10 Los Angeles Lakers
The celebrity fans might get the attention, but the Lakers have plenty of loud supporters sitting higher up at Staples Center.

Photo Credits

Cover: Greg Nelson for Sports Illustrated
Back Cover: Issac Baldizon/Getty Images (Wade/James); Dutch Zacharitas (Sneaker); Fernando Medina/Getty Images (McGrady); Rocky Widner/Getty Images (Bogues); Nathaniel S. Butler/Getty Images (Jordan)
Title Page: Andrew D. Bernstein/Getty Images
Copyright Page: Nathaniel S. Butler/Getty Images
Table of Contents: Brian Babineau/Getty Images
Greatest Players: Chris Graythen/Getty Images (James); Nathaniel S. Butler/Getty Images (Jordan); Dick Raphael/Getty Images (Russell, Bird, Chamberlain); Reed Saxon/AP Images (Johnson); Focus On Sport/Getty Images (Robertson); Richard Mackson/Getty Images (Abdul-Jabbar); Mike Ehrmann/Getty Images (Duncan); Cameron Browne/Getty Images (Bryant)
Teams: Getty Images (1995–96 Bulls, 1971–72 Lakers, 1966–67 Sixers, 1985–86 Celtics, 1982–83 Sixers, 1970–71 Bucks, 1986–87 Lakers); Andrew D. Bernstein/Getty Images (1999–2000 Lakers); Brian Babineau/Getty Images (2006–07 Celtics); Issac Baldizon/Getty Images (2012–13 Heat)
Hairstyles: Jonathan Daniel/Getty Images (Wallace, Noah); Rocky Widner/Getty Images (Anderson); Mike Powell/Getty Images (Walker); Garrett Ellwood/Getty Images (Iverson); Jon SooHoo/Getty Images (Schintzius); Jeff Haynes/Getty Images (Rodman); Anonymous/AP Images (Bynum); Stephen Dunn/Getty Images (World Peace); Timothy A. Clary/Getty Images (Gooden)
International Stars: Joe Murphy/Getty Images (Nowitzki); Bill Baptist/Getty Images (Parker); Rocky Widner/Getty Images (Ming, Petrovic, Divac); Victor Decolongon/Getty Images (Gasol); Andy Lyons/Getty Images (Ginobili); Layne Murdoch/Getty Images (Stojakovic); Contributor (The Sporting News)/Getty Images (Kukoc); Robert Skeoch/Getty Images (Sabonis)
Coolest Jerseys: Brian Drake/Getty Images (Nuggets); Fernando Medina/Getty Images (Raptors); Jamie Squire/Getty Images (Hawks); Rocky Widner/Getty Images (Bucks, Sonics, Cavaliers); Sam Forencich/Getty Images (Blazers); Nathaniel S. Butler/Getty Images (Sixers); Joe Murphy/Getty Images (Rockets); Andy Hayt/Getty Images (Jazz)
Greatest Duos: Andy Hayt/Getty Images (Jordan/Pippen); Andrew D. Bernstein/Getty Images (Bryant/O'Neal, Bird/McHale); Norm Perdue/Getty Images (Stockton/Malone); Focus On Sport/Getty Images (Johnson/Abdul-Jabbar); Nathaniel S. Butler/Getty Images (James/Wade, Thomas/Dumars); Dick Raphael/Getty Images (Abdul-Jabbar/Robertson); Contributor/Getty Images (Cousy/Russell); Associated Press/AP Images (Reed/Frazier)
Trades: Herb Shartman/Getty Images (Russell); Focus On Sport/Getty Images (Abdul-Jabbar); Dick Raphael/Getty Images (Robertson, Parish, Chamberlain, Wilkins); Nathaniel S. Butler/Getty Images (Garnett); Noren Trotman/Getty Images (Barkley); Harry How/Getty Images (Gasol)
NBA Finals Games: Noah Graham/Getty Images (Spurs/Heat 2013); Nathaniel S. Butler/Getty Images (Bulls/Jazz 1997, Sixers/Lakers 2001); Dick Raphael/Getty Images (Suns/Celtics 1976); Boston Globe/Getty Images (Hawks/Celtics 1957); Associated Press/AP Images (Lakers/Celtics 1962, Knicks/Lakers 1970, Celtics/Lakers 1969); Ronald Martinez/Getty Images (Celtics/Lakers 2010); Sun Sentinel/Getty Images (Mavericks/Heat 2011);
WNBA Players: Andrew D. Bernstein/Getty Images (Leslie, Parker); Kellie Landis/Getty Images (Cooper); D. Clarke Evans/Getty Images (Jackson); Barry Gossage/Getty Images (Swoopes, Taurasi); David Dow/Getty Images (Catchings); Terrence Vaccaro/Getty Images (Thompson, Bird); Nathaniel S. Butler/Getty Images (Pondexter)
Quotes/Sneakers: Al Behrman/AP Images (Bird); Damian Dovarganes/AP Images (Divac); Rich Pedroncelli/AP Images (Malone); Evan Agostini/AP Images (Barkley); Ann Heisenfelt/AP Images (Tomjanovich); Lynne Sladky/AP Images (O'Neal); Focus On Sport/Getty Images (Chamberlain); Andy Hayt/Getty Images (Rodman); Mike Ehrmann/Getty Images (James); Andrew D. Bernstein/Getty Images (Jordan); Dutch Zacharitas (Sneakers)
Game Winning Shots: Ed Wagner/Getty Images (Jordan); Andrew D. Bernstein/Getty Images (Fisher, Bryant, Sampson); Jeff Haynes/Getty Images (Jordan); Brian Drake/Getty Images (Johnson); Dick Raphael/Getty Images (Johnson); Cameron Browne/Getty Images (Lillard); Harry How/Getty Images (Horry); Noah Graham/Getty Images (Artest)
Nicknames: Dick Raphael/Getty Images (Dawkins, Gervin, Erving, Maravich); Andrew D. Bernstein/Getty Images (Malone); Focus On Sport/Getty Images (Robertson); Jared Wickerham/Getty Images (Pierce); Gregory Shamus/Getty Images (Payton, Iverson); Jeff Haynes/Getty Images (Olajuwon)
Mascots: Randy Belice/Getty Images (Benny the Bull); Barry Gossage/Getty Images (Go the Gorilla); Layne Murdoch/Getty Images (Rumble the Bison, Hugo the Hornet); Garrett Ellwood/Getty Images (Rocky the Mountain Lion); Gary Dineen/Getty Images (Bango the Buck); Terrence Vaccaro/Getty Images (Squatch); Joe Murphy/Getty Images (Grizz); Ned Dishman/Getty Images (G-Man); Scott Cunningham/Getty Images (Harry the Hawk); The Image Bank/Getty Images (Court Image)
Draft Steals: D. Clarke Evans/Getty Images (Ginobili); Andrew D. Bernstein/Getty Images (English); Dick Raphael/Getty Images (Johnson); Brian Drake/Getty Images (Rodman); Gregory Shamus/Getty Images (Arenas); Fernando Medina/Getty Images (Lewis, Redd); Joe Murphy/Getty Images (Gasol); Focus On Sport/Getty Images (Archibald); Tom DeFrisco/Getty Images (Petrovic)
Draft Busts: Allen Einstein/Getty Images (Milicic); Brian Drake/Getty Images (Bowie); Brian Babineau/Getty Images (Morrison); Cameron Browne/Getty Images (Oden); Noah Graham/Getty Images (Olowokandi); Garrett Ellwood/

Getty Images (Brown); Rocky Widner/Getty Images (Ferry, Ellison); NBA Photos/Getty Images (Martin); Joe Murphy/Getty Images (Thabeet)
Clutch Players: Nathaniel S. Butler/Getty Images (Jordan); Focus On Sport/Getty Images (West); Mark Duncan/AP Images (Bird); Stephen Dunn/Getty Images (Bryant, Johnson); Andrew D. Bernstein/Getty Images (Horry); Noren Trotman/Getty Images (Miller); Noah Graham/Getty Images (Pierce); Dick Raphael/Getty Images (Havlicek); Allen Einstein/Getty Images (Billups)
Future Stars: Layne Murdoch Jr./Getty Images (Davis); David Liam Kyle/Getty Images (Irving); Ed Zurga/Getty Images (Wiggins, Embiid); Ned Dishman/Getty Images (Beal); Streeter Lecka/Getty Images (Parker); Allen Einstein/Getty Images (Drummond); Kelly Kline/Getty Images (Okafor); Ron Turenne/Getty Images (Valanciunas); Rocky Widner/Getty Images (Antetokounmpo)
Scorers: Lennox Mclendon/AP Images (Abdul-Jabbar); Andy Hayt/Getty Images (Malone, Iverson); Frank Gunn/AP Images (Jordan); Stephen Dunn/Getty Images (Bryant); Ken Regan/Getty Images (Chamberlain); Ned Dishman/Getty Images (Durant); Dick Raphael/Getty Images (Baylor, McAdoo); Fred Jewell/AP Images (Gervin)
Defenders: Focus On Sport/Getty Images (Russell); Bob Rosato/Sports Illustrated (Howard); David Dow/Getty Images (Garnett); Elsa/Getty Images (Wallace); Andrew D. Bernstein/Getty Images (Cooper, Mutombo, Moncrief); Stephen Dunn/Getty Images (Eaton); Brian Babineau/Getty Images (Payton); Matt Campbell/Getty Images (Olajuwon)
Dunkers: Andrew D. Bernstein/Getty Images (Carter, Jordan); Don Larson/AP Images (Wilkins); NBA Photos/Getty Images (Erving); Jesse D. Garrabrant/Getty Images (Howard); Andy Hayt/Getty Images (Miner); Kevork Djansezian/Getty Images (Griffin); Mike Powell/Getty Images (Webb); Ronald Martinez/Getty Images (Robinson); Nathaniel S. Butler/Getty Images (Richardson)
Big Guys: Dick Raphael/Getty Images (Chamberlain, Gilmore); Bill Baptist/Getty Images (Abdul-Jabbar); Andrew D. Bernstein/Getty Images (O'Neal); Glenn James/Getty Images (Nowitzki); Jesse D. Garrabrant/Getty Images (Robinson); Rocky Widner/Getty Images (Ewing, Parish); Stephen Dunn/Getty Images (Ming); Scott Cunningham/Getty Images (Mutombo)
Little Guys: Jonathan Daniel/Getty Images (Iverson); Dick Raphael/Getty Images (Thomas, Murphy); Barry Gossage/Getty Images (Nash); Noah Graham/Getty Images (Paul); Nathaniel S. Butler/Getty Images (Price); Garrett Ellwood/Getty Images (Lawson); Rocky Widner/Getty Images (Webb); Todd Warshaw/Getty Images (Bogues); Fernando Medina/Getty Images (Robinson)
High School to NBA: Bob Leverone TSN/Getty Images (James); Doug Pensinger/Getty Images (Bryant); Andy Hayt/NBAE/Getty Images (O'Neal); Carl Sissac/Getty Images (Garnett); Jeff Haynes/Getty Images (Howard); Sheedy & Long for Sports Illustrated (Malone); Fernando Medina/Getty Images (McGrady); Andrew D. Bernstein/Getty Images (Stoudemire); Dick Raphael/Getty Images (Dawkins); Nathaniel S. Butler/Getty Images (Smith)

Single-Game Regular-Season Performances: Paul Vathis/AP Images (Chamberlain); Andrew D. Bernstein/Getty Images (Malone, Robinson); Dick Raphael/Getty Images (Thurmond); Noah Graham/Getty Images (Bryant); Nathaniel S. Butler/Getty Images (Skiles, Jordan); David Sherman/Getty Images (Love); NBA Photos/Getty Images (Thompson); Focus On Sport/Getty Images (Chamberlain)
Families: Andrew D. Bernstein/Getty Images (Brent/Rick Barry, Kobe/Joe Bryant, Stephen/Dell/Seth Curry, Bill/Luke Walton, Marc/Pau Gasol); Rocky Widner/Getty Images (Jon Barry); Gary Dineen/Getty Images (Reggie and Cheryl Miller); Nathaniel S. Butler/Getty Images (Dominique/Gerald Wilkins); Garrett Ellwood/Getty Images (Stan/Kevin Love); Bob Gomel/Getty Images (Tom/Dick Van Arsdale)
Sixth Men: Rocky Widner/Getty Images (Ginobili, Pierce); Dick Raphael/Getty Images (McHale); Layne Murdoch/Getty Images (Harden); Nathaniel S. Butler/Getty Images (Schrempf); NBA Photos/Getty Images (Robinson); Ronald Martinez/Getty Images (Terry); Scott Cunningham/Getty Images (Crawford); Getty Images/Getty Images (Johnson); New York Daily News Archive/Getty Images (Starks)
Rebounders: Dick Raphael/Getty Images (Chamberlain, Russell, Pettit); Andy Hayt/Getty Images (Rodman, Barkley); Focus On Sport/Getty Images (Malone); Jesse D. Garrabrant/Getty Images (Howard); Rocky Widner/Getty Images (Love); Jerry Wachter/Getty Images (Unseld); Lou Capozzola for Sports Illustrated (Garnett)
Shooters: Rocky Widner/Getty Images (Curry, Stojakovic, Kerr); Jesse D. Garrabrant/Getty Images (Allen, Korver); The Sporting News/Getty Images (Miller); Glenn James/Getty Images (Nash); Focus On Sport/Getty Images (Bird); Danny Bollinger/Getty Images (Nowitzki); Andrew D. Bernstein/Getty Images (Hodges); Ryan McVay/Getty Images (Swish); Steve Greer/Getty Images (Image)
Single-Game Postseason Performances: Andy Hayt/Getty Images (Jordan); Focus On Sport/Getty Images (Johnson); Elise Amendola/AP Images (James); Lou Capozzola/Getty Images (Miller); Robert Riger/Getty Images (Russell); Sam Forencich/Getty Images (Barkley); Dick Raphael/Getty Images (Baylor, Jordan); The Stevenson Collection/Getty Images (Pettit); Nathaniel S. Butler/Getty Images (James)
Triple-Double Threats: Dick Raphael/Getty Images (Robertson, Havlicek); Andrew D. Bernstein/Getty Images (Johnson, Lever); Noah Graham/Getty Images (Kidd); Ken Regan/Getty Images (Chamberlain); Scott Cunningham/Getty Images (Bird, James); Ezra Shaw/Getty Images (Hill); Robert Lewis/Getty Images (Jordan)
Fans: Rocky Widner/Getty Images (Kings); Nam Y. Huh/AP Images (Bulls); Joe Murphy/Getty Images (Spurs); Brett Deering/Getty Images (Thunder); Christian Petersen/Getty Images (Suns); Boston Globe/Getty Images (Celtics); Garrett Ellwood/Getty Images (Warriors); Melissa Majchrzak/Getty Images (Jazz); Ronald Martinez/Getty Images (Mavericks); Noah Graham/Getty Images (Lakers)